The
Placebo
Man

Tomer Hanuka

The Placebo Man

Tomer Hanuka

The Placebo Man
Tomer Hanuka

The stories presented here were originally serialized in issues one through five of the comic book series Bipolar, except Elephant Graveyard which was first published in New Thing: Identity, an anthology edited by Jim Higgins.

The Placebo Man. ISBN: 1-891867-91-1

Printed in Canada February 2006.

Alternative Comics
503 NW 37th Avenue
Gainesville, FL 32609-2204
Phone: (352) 373-6336
jmason@indyworld.com
www.indyworld.com

Design: **Kobi Franco**
Language Editor: **Thomas Herpich**

Special thanks to Jeff Mason, Asaf Hanuka, Etgar Keret, Tal Sharon, Thomas Herpich, James Jean, Esao Andrews, Farel Dalrymple, Brandon Graham, Alex Holden, GB Tran, Dean Haspiel, Jessica Abel, Matt Madden and Karen Oxman.

www.thanuka.com

"That's how it is. You yearn
for someone, maniacally,
mortally, to the verge of hell
and death. You look for them
everywhere, pursue them, to
no avail, and your life wastes
away in nostalgia"

Antal Szerb, Journey by Moonlight

For Karen

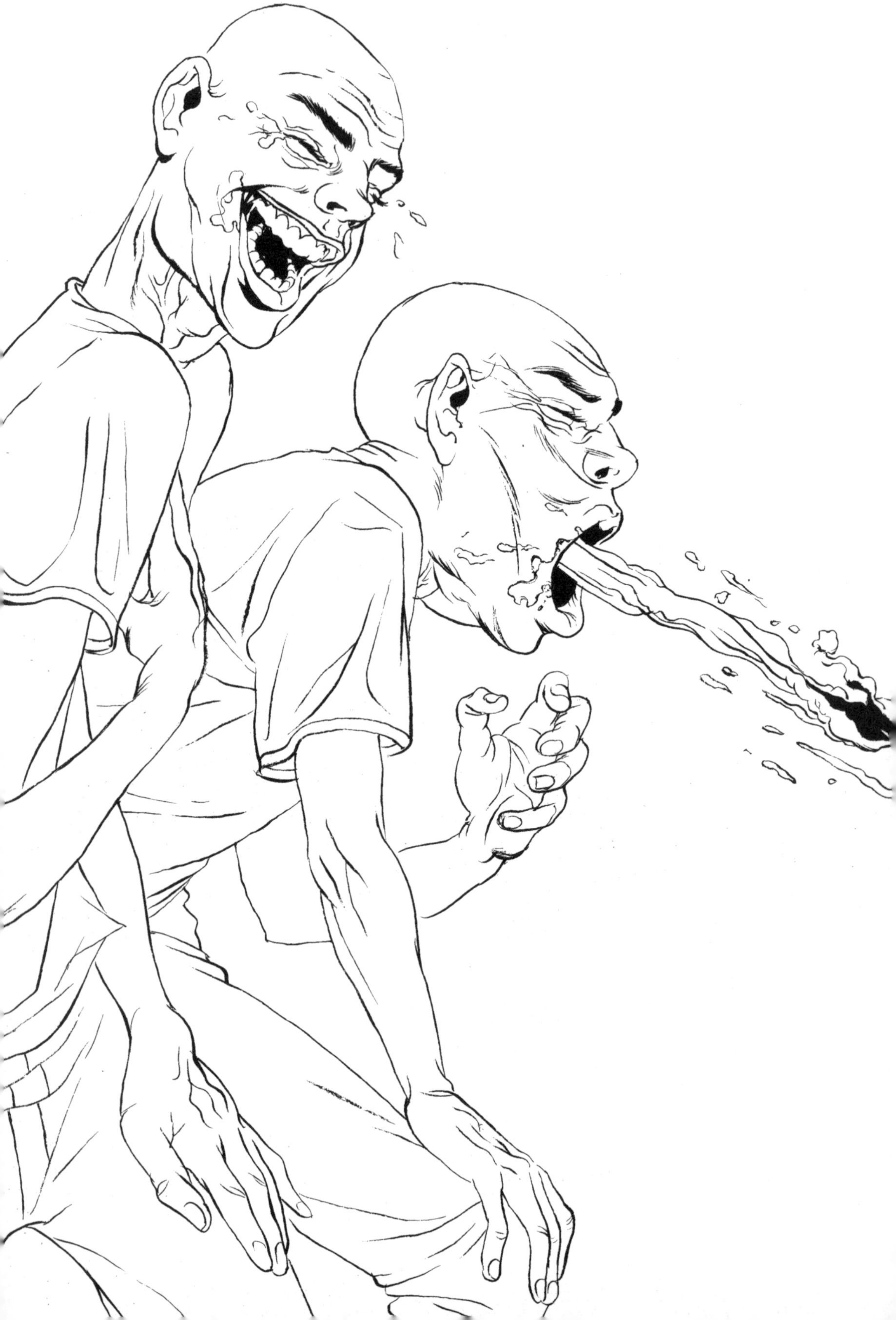

Time Strips

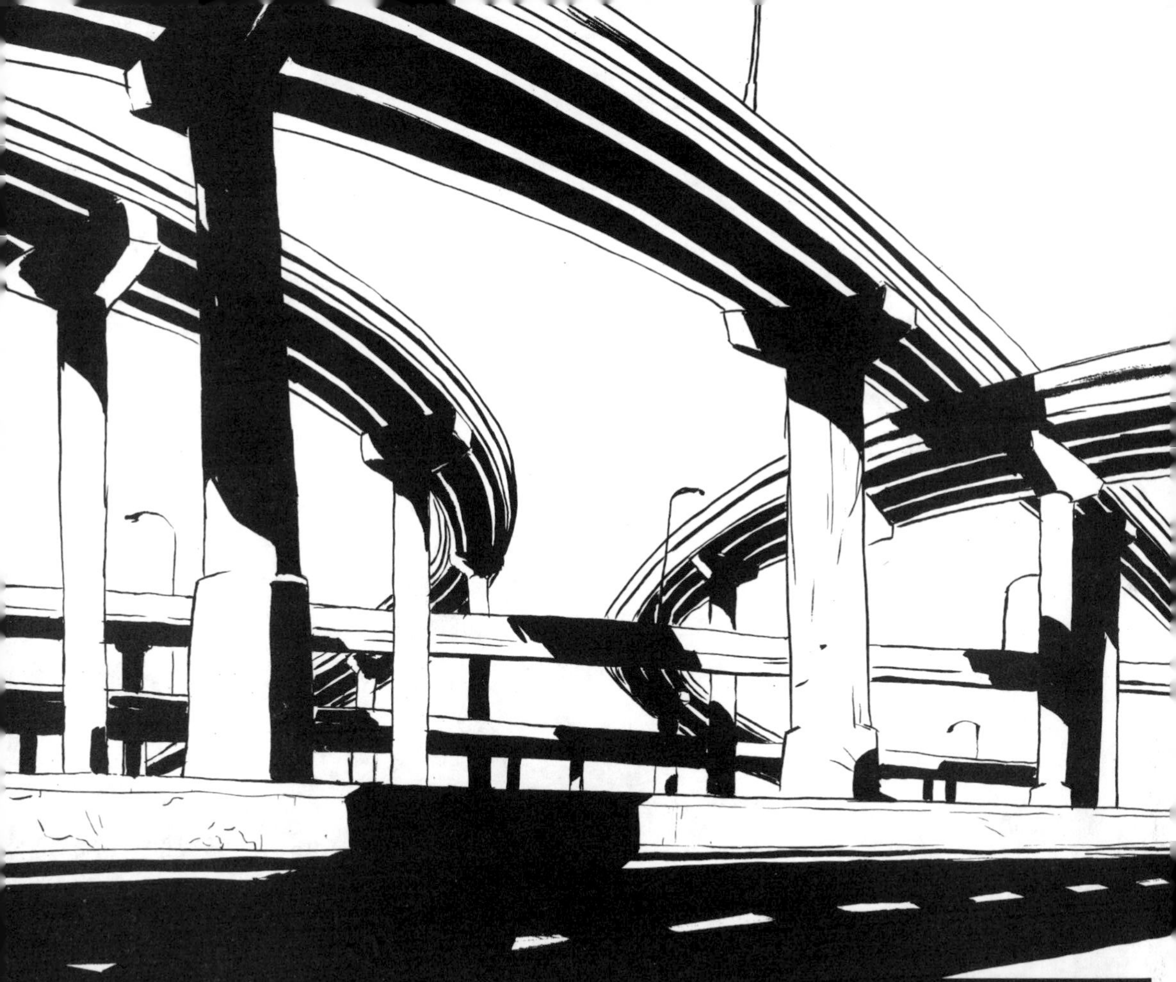
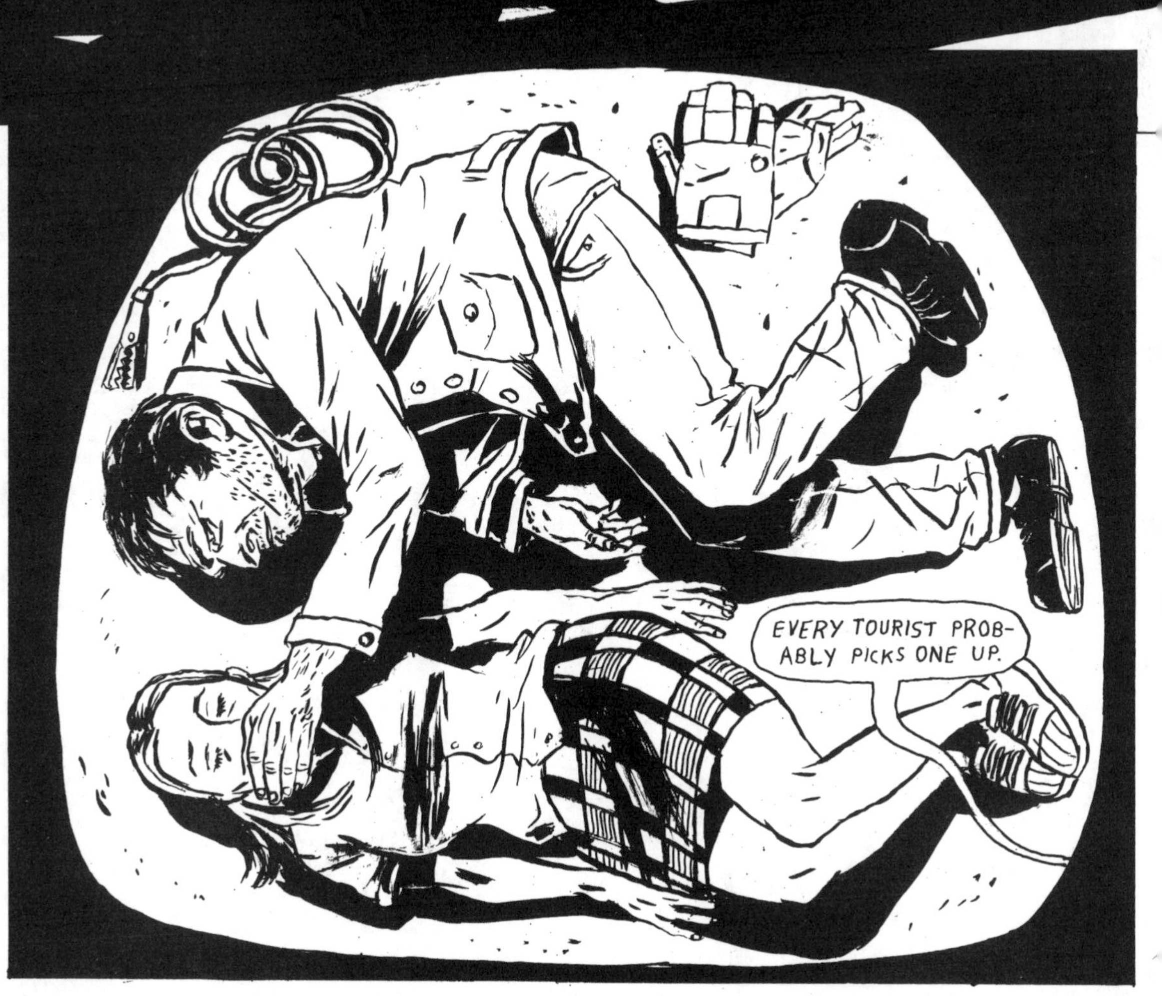
EVERY TOURIST PROB-
ABLY PICKS ONE UP.

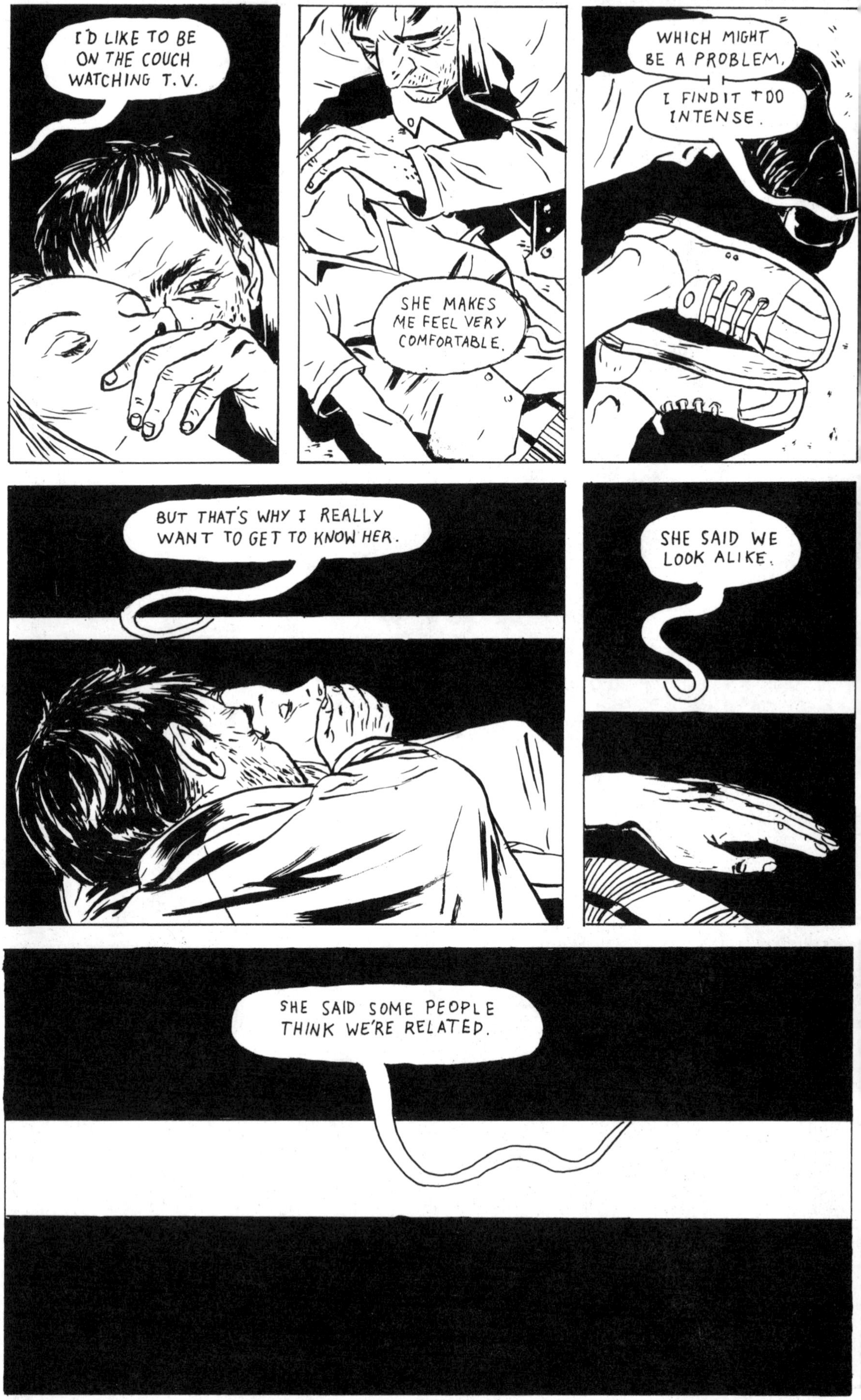
I'D LIKE TO BE ON THE COUCH WATCHING T.V.
SHE MAKES ME FEEL VERY COMFORTABLE.
WHICH MIGHT BE A PROBLEM,
I FINDIT TOO INTENSE.
BUT THAT'S WHY I REALLY WANT TO GET TO KNOW HER.
SHE SAID WE LOOK ALIKE.
SHE SAID SOME PEOPLE THINK WE'RE RELATED.

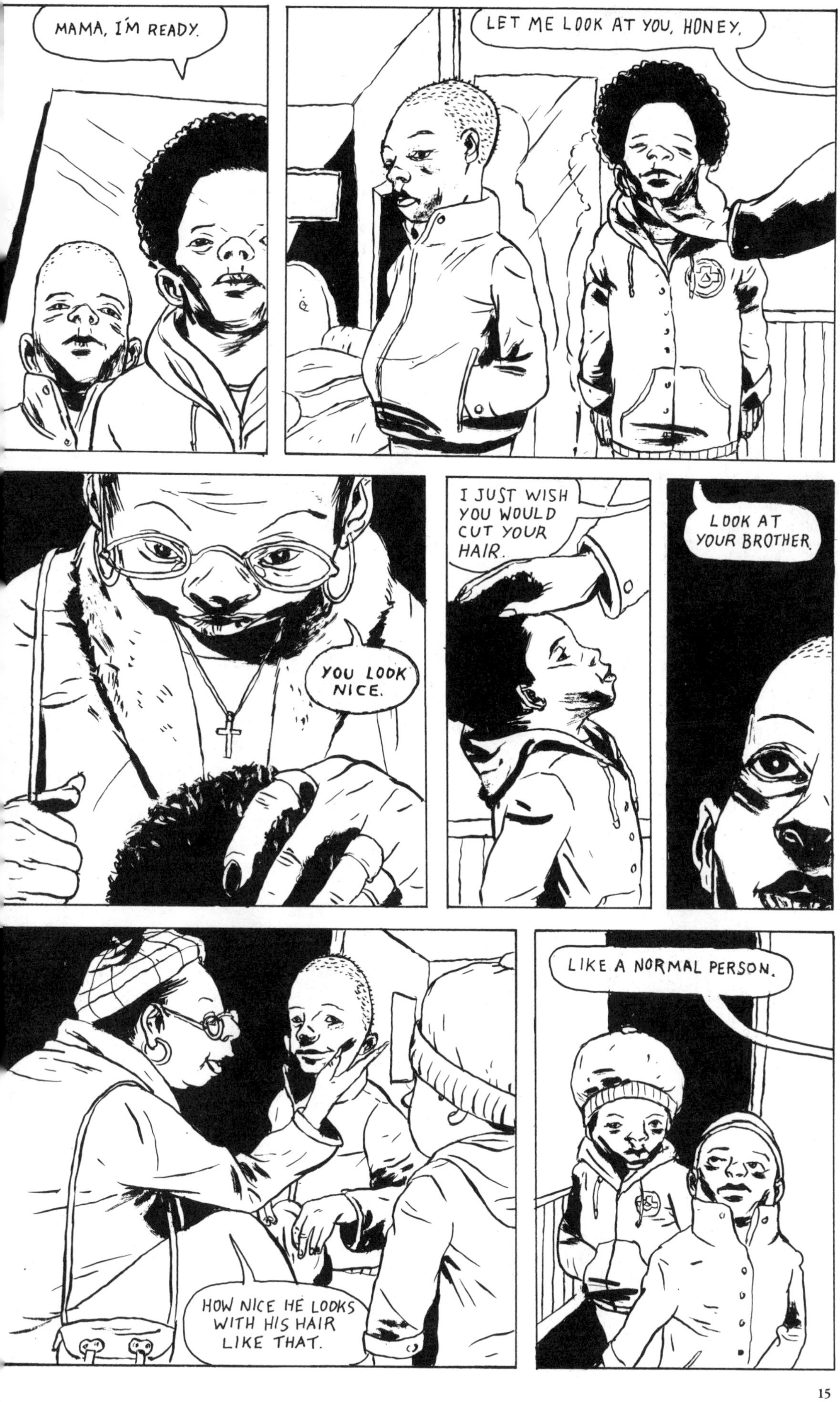
MAMA, I'M READY.
LET ME LOOK AT YOU, HONEY.
YOU LOOK NICE.
I JUST WISH YOU WOULD CUT YOUR HAIR.
LOOK AT YOUR BROTHER.
HOW NICE HE LOOKS WITH HIS HAIR LIKE THAT.
LIKE A NORMAL PERSON.

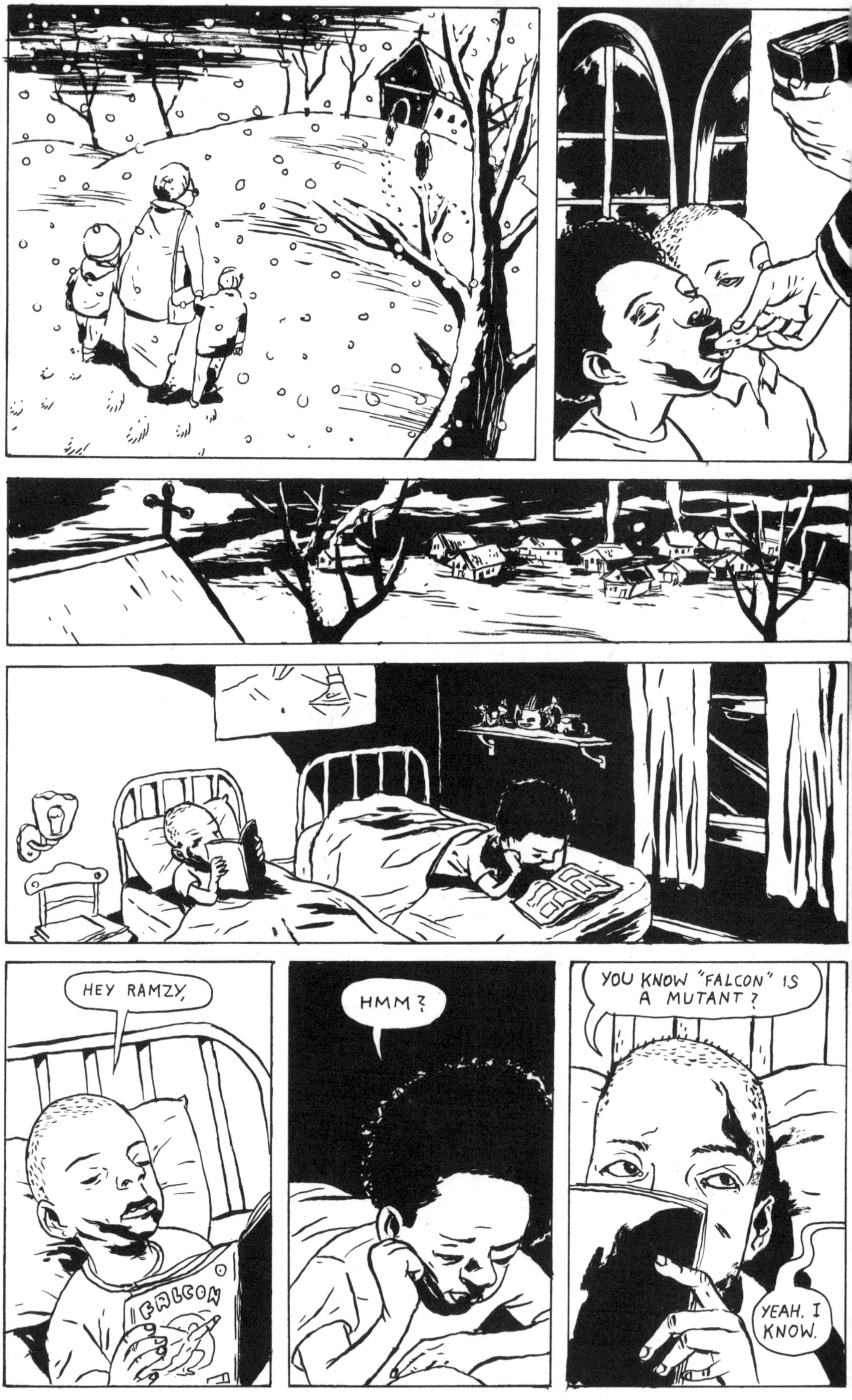
HEY RAMZY,
HMM?
YOU KNOW "FALCON" IS A MUTANT?
YEAH, I KNOW.
FALCON

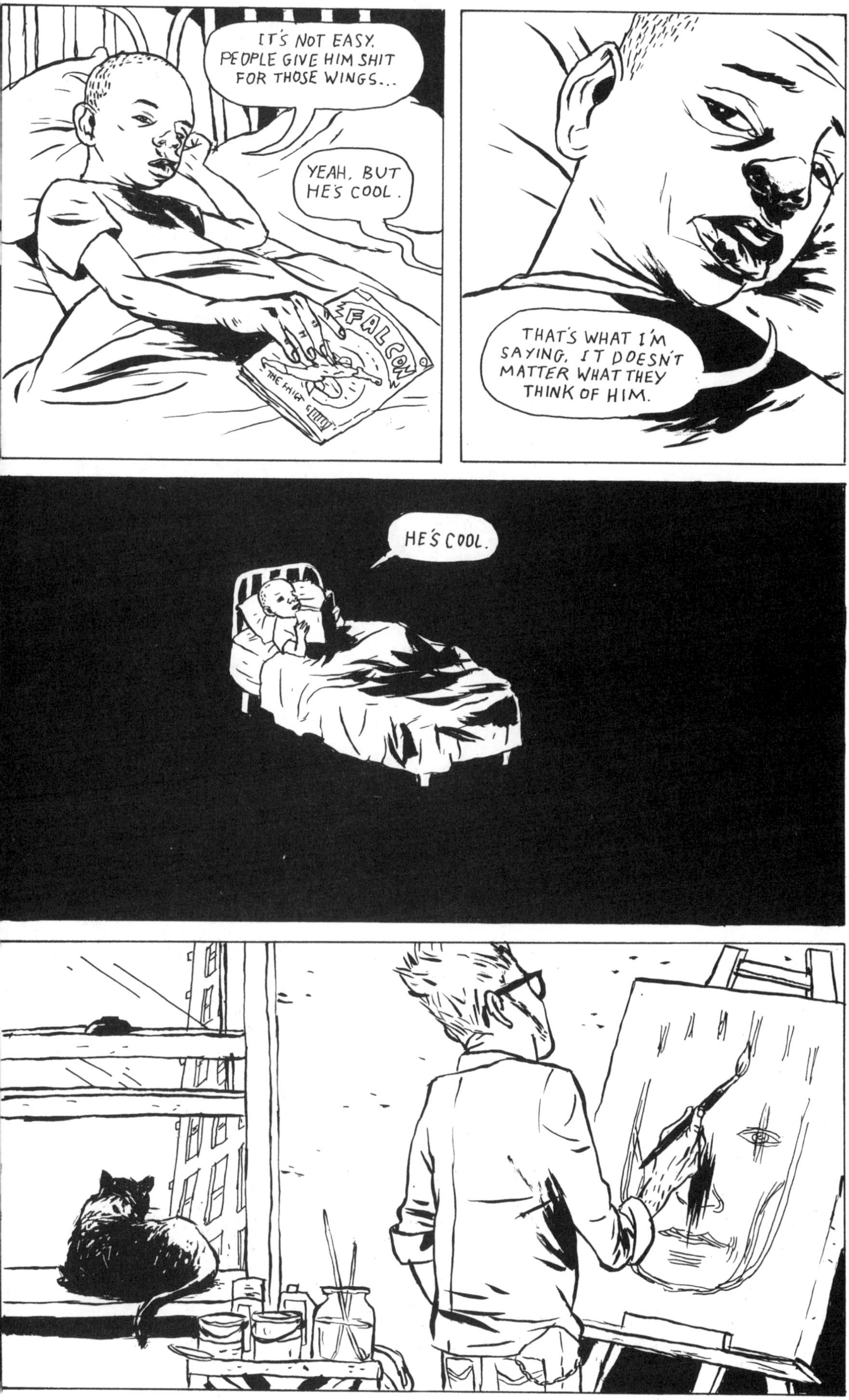
IT'S NOT EASY. PEOPLE GIVE HIM SHIT FOR THOSE WINGS...
YEAH, BUT HE'S COOL.
FALCON
THAT'S WHAT I'M SAYING. IT DOESN'T MATTER WHAT THEY THINK OF HIM.
HE'S COOL.

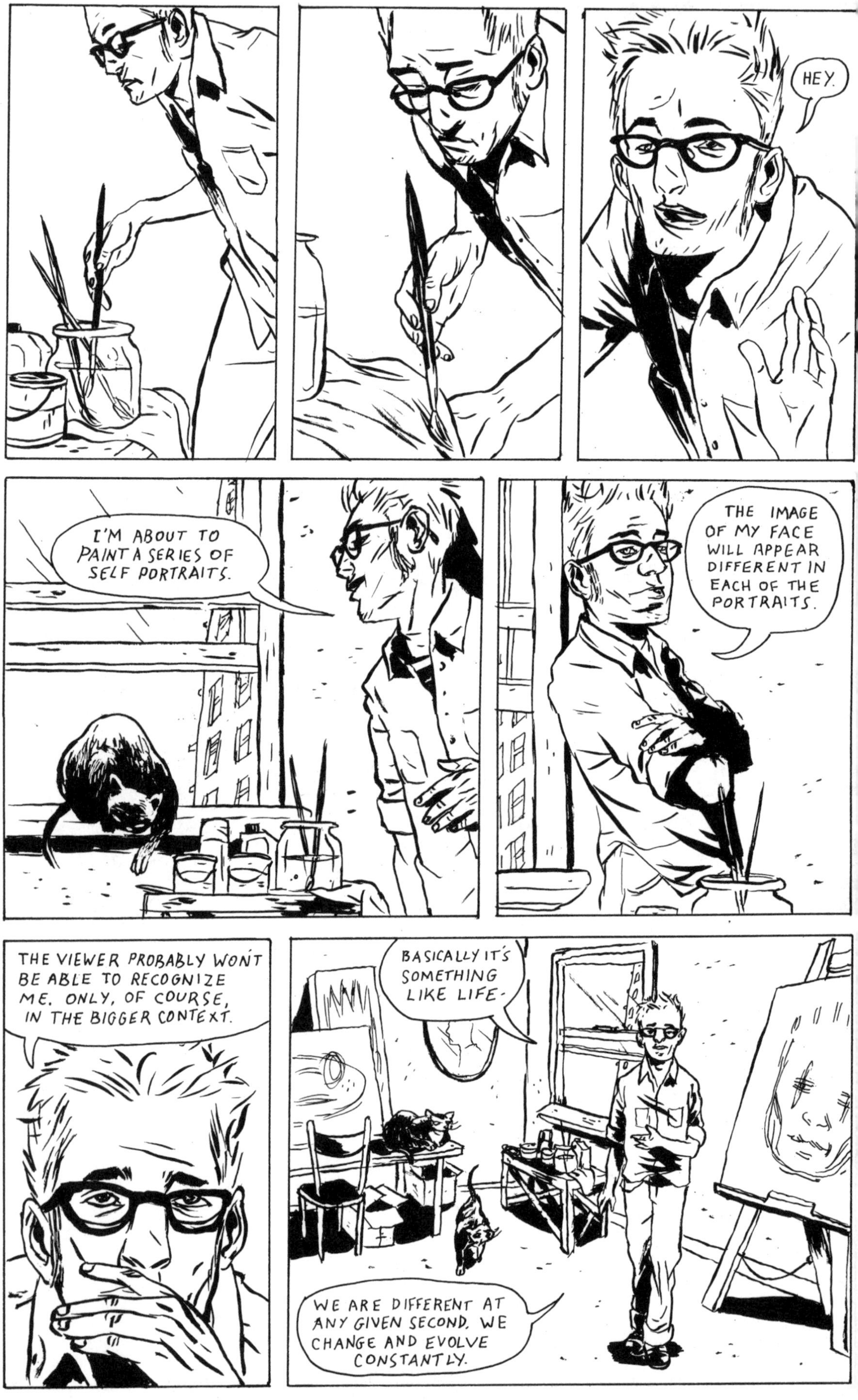
HEY.
I'M ABOUT TO PAINT A SERIES OF SELF PORTRAITS.
THE IMAGE OF MY FACE WILL APPEAR DIFFERENT IN EACH OF THE PORTRAITS.
THE VIEWER PROBABLY WON'T BE ABLE TO RECOGNIZE ME. ONLY, OF COURSE, IN THE BIGGER CONTEXT.
BASICALLY IT'S SOMETHING LIKE LIFE-
WE ARE DIFFERENT AT ANY GIVEN SECOND. WE CHANGE AND EVOLVE CONSTANTLY.

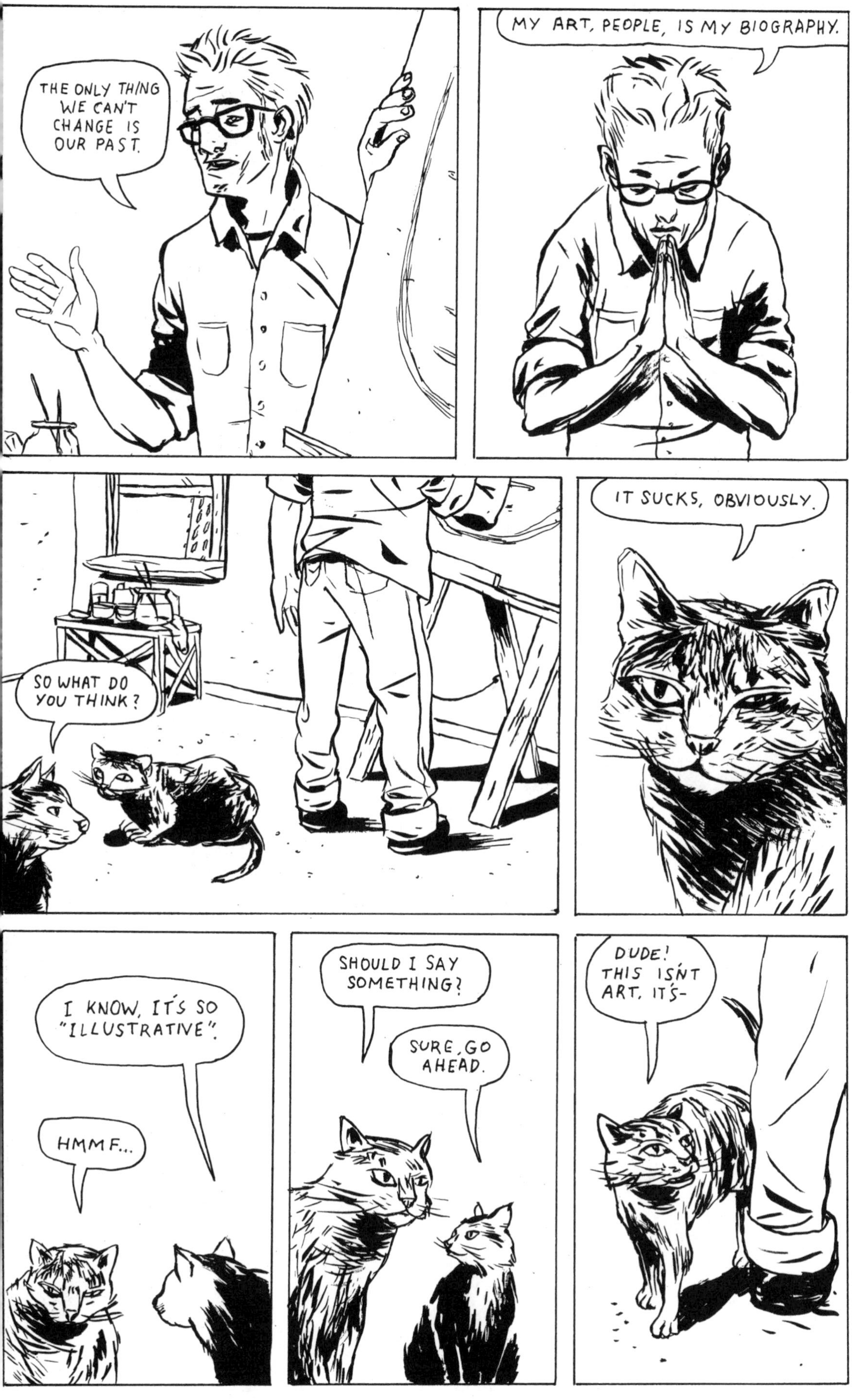
THE ONLY THING WE CAN'T CHANGE IS OUR PAST.
MY ART, PEOPLE, IS MY BIOGRAPHY.
SO WHAT DO YOU THINK?
IT SUCKS, OBVIOUSLY.
I KNOW, IT'S SO "ILLUSTRATIVE".
HMMF...
SHOULD I SAY SOMETHING?
SURE, GO AHEAD.
DUDE! THIS ISN'T ART, IT'S-

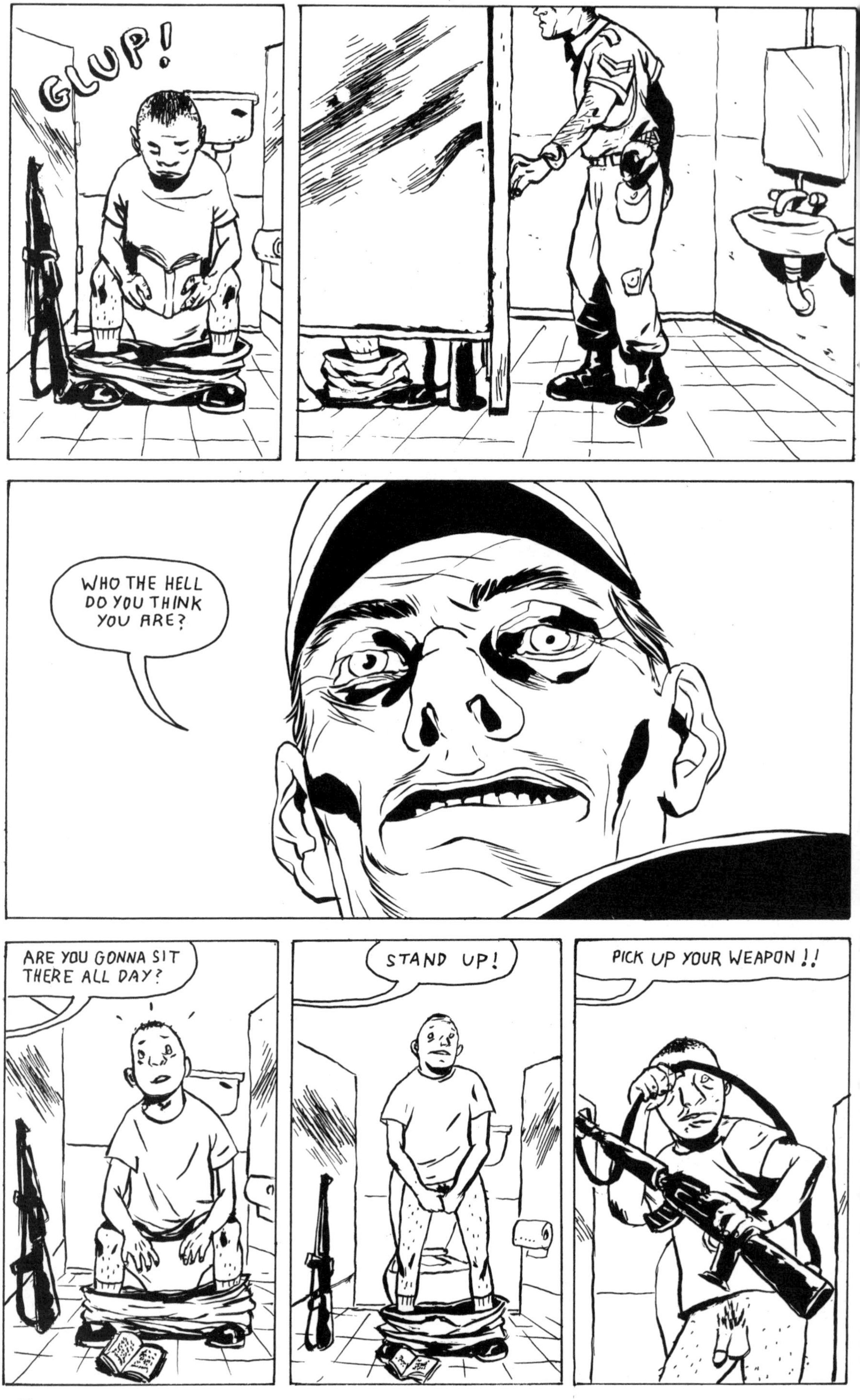
GLUP!
WHO THE HELL DO YOU THINK YOU ARE?
ARE YOU GONNA SIT THERE ALL DAY?
STAND UP!
PICK UP YOUR WEAPON!!

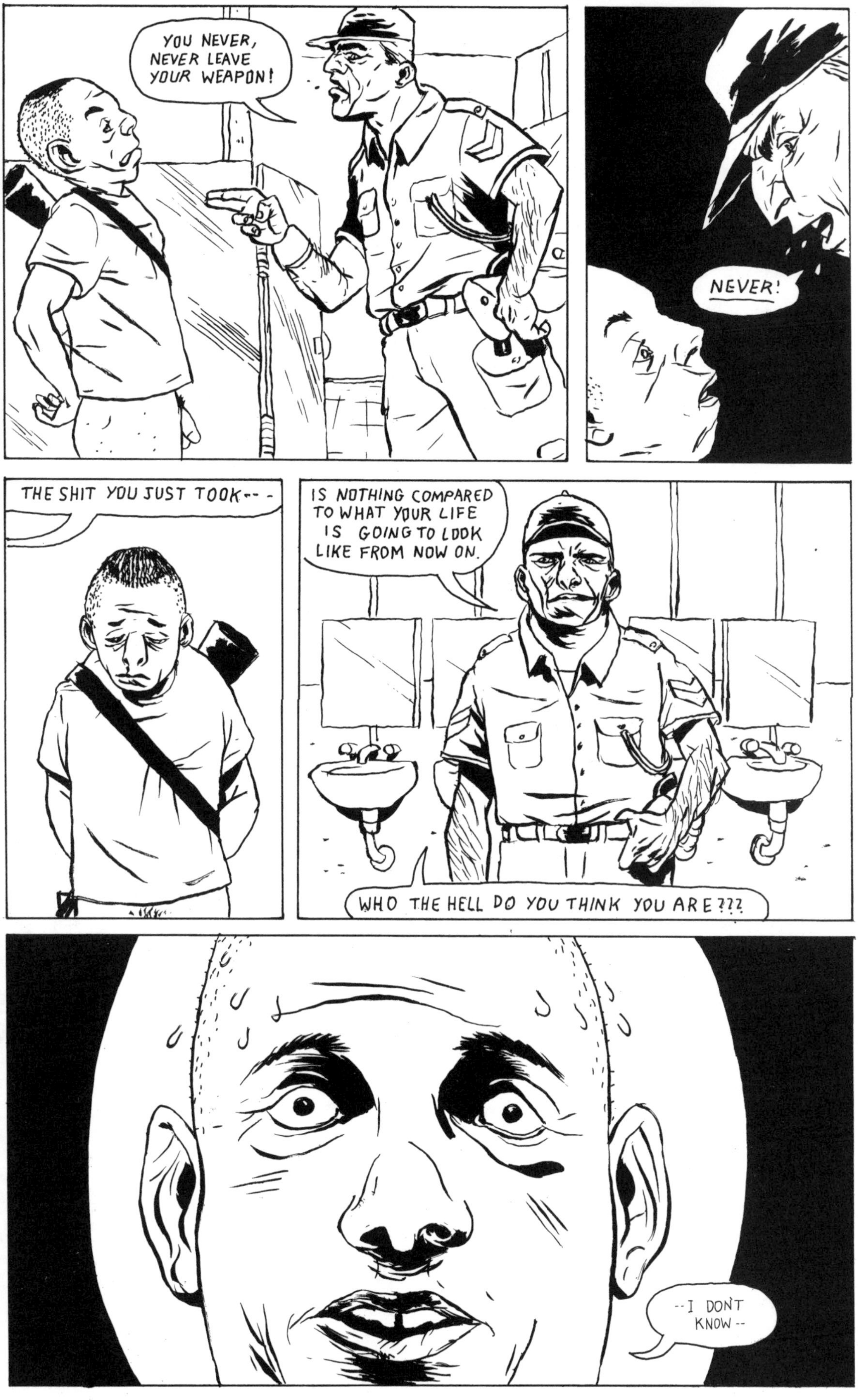
YOU NEVER, NEVER LEAVE YOUR WEAPON!
NEVER!
THE SHIT YOU JUST TOOK---
IS NOTHING COMPARED TO WHAT YOUR LIFE IS GOING TO LOOK LIKE FROM NOW ON.
WHO THE HELL DO YOU THINK YOU ARE???
--I DON'T KNOW--

FFFT

PERFECT!

BZZZ...

DON'T SAY A WORD.

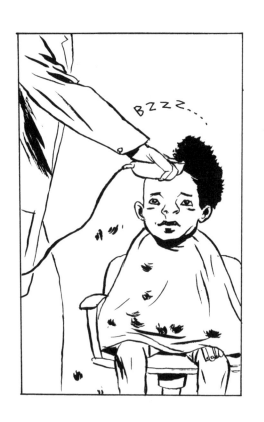

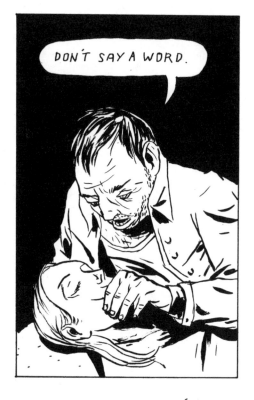

(THE END)

I Love You

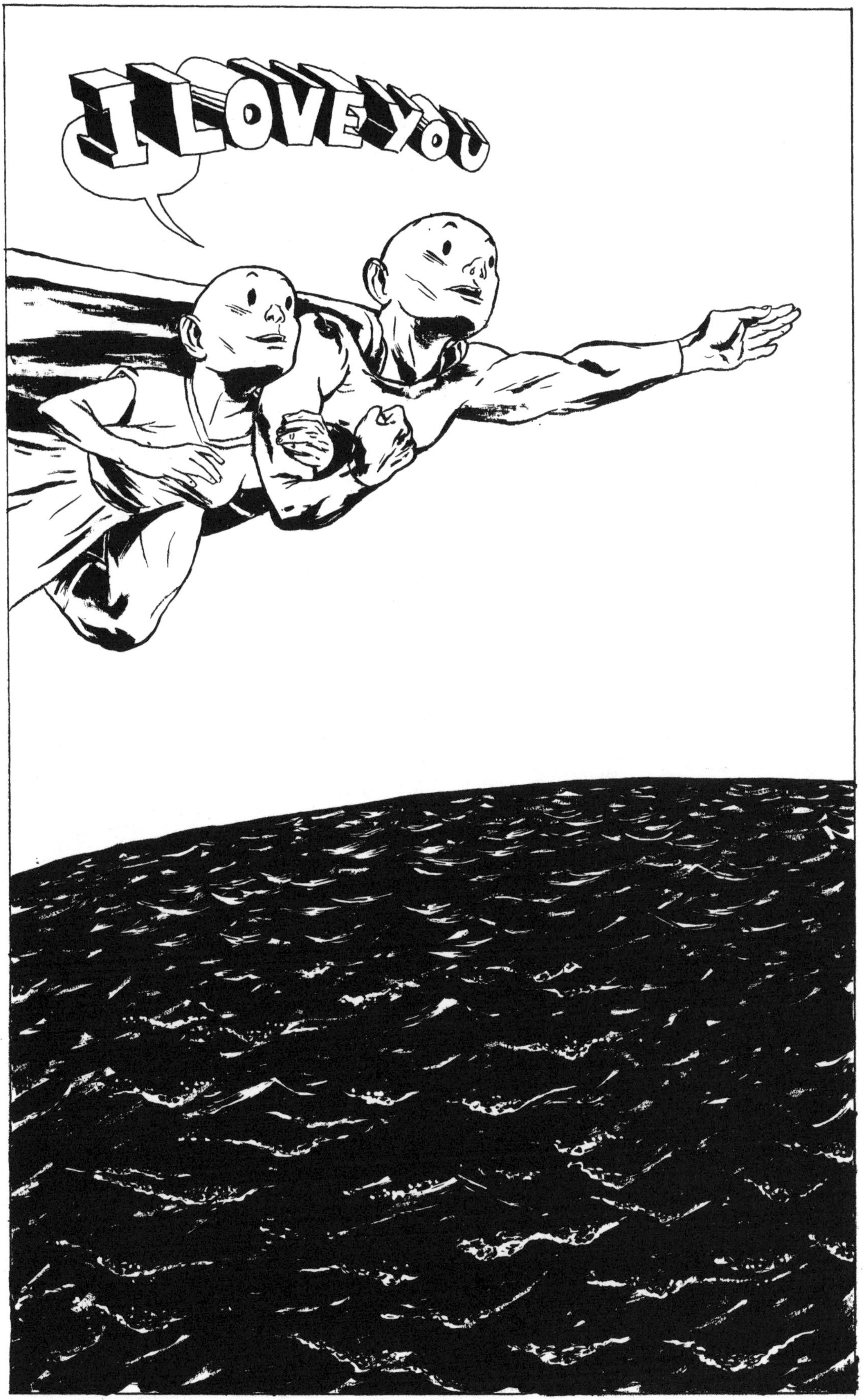
I LOVE YOU

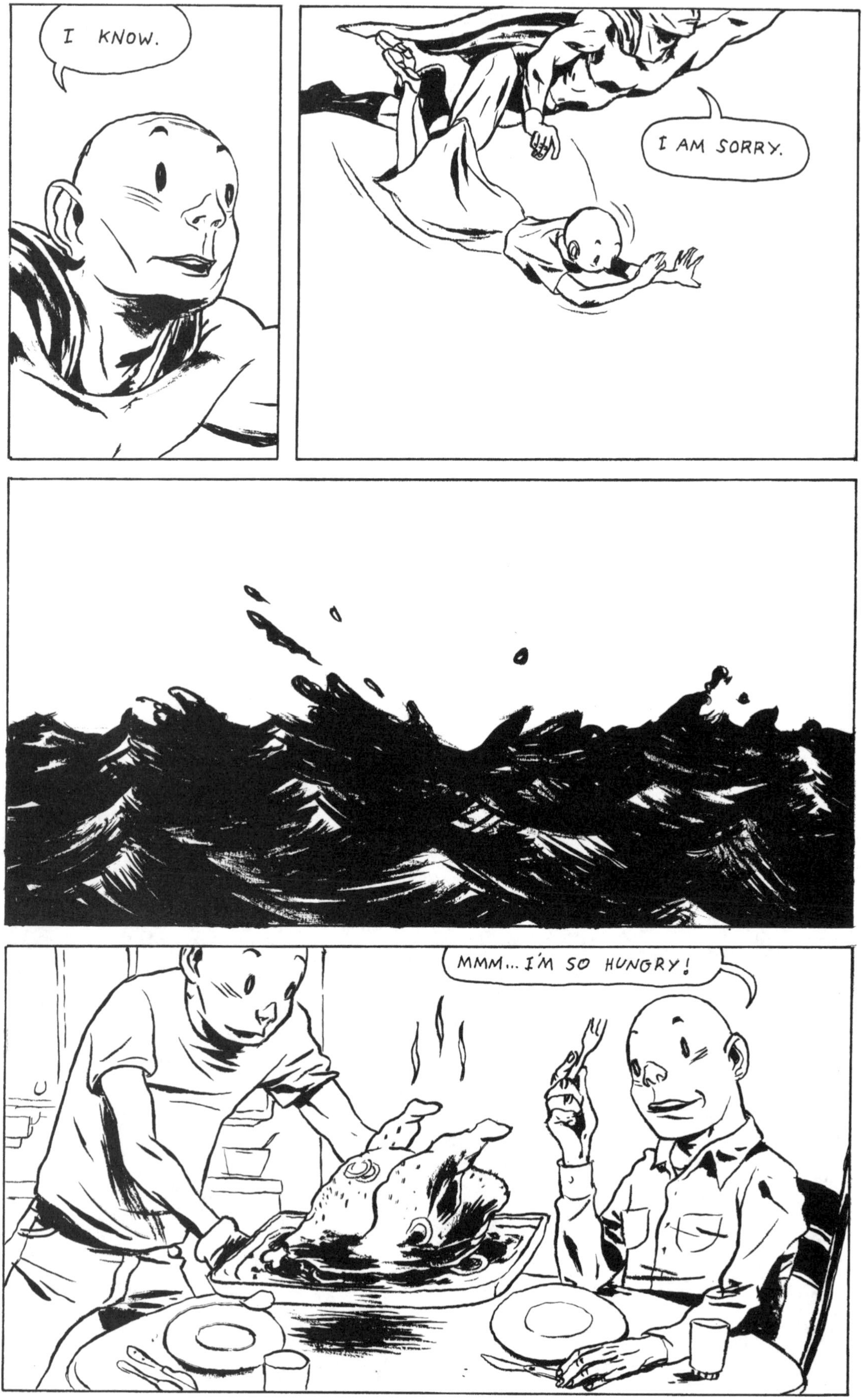
I KNOW.
I AM SORRY.
MMM... I'M SO HUNGRY!

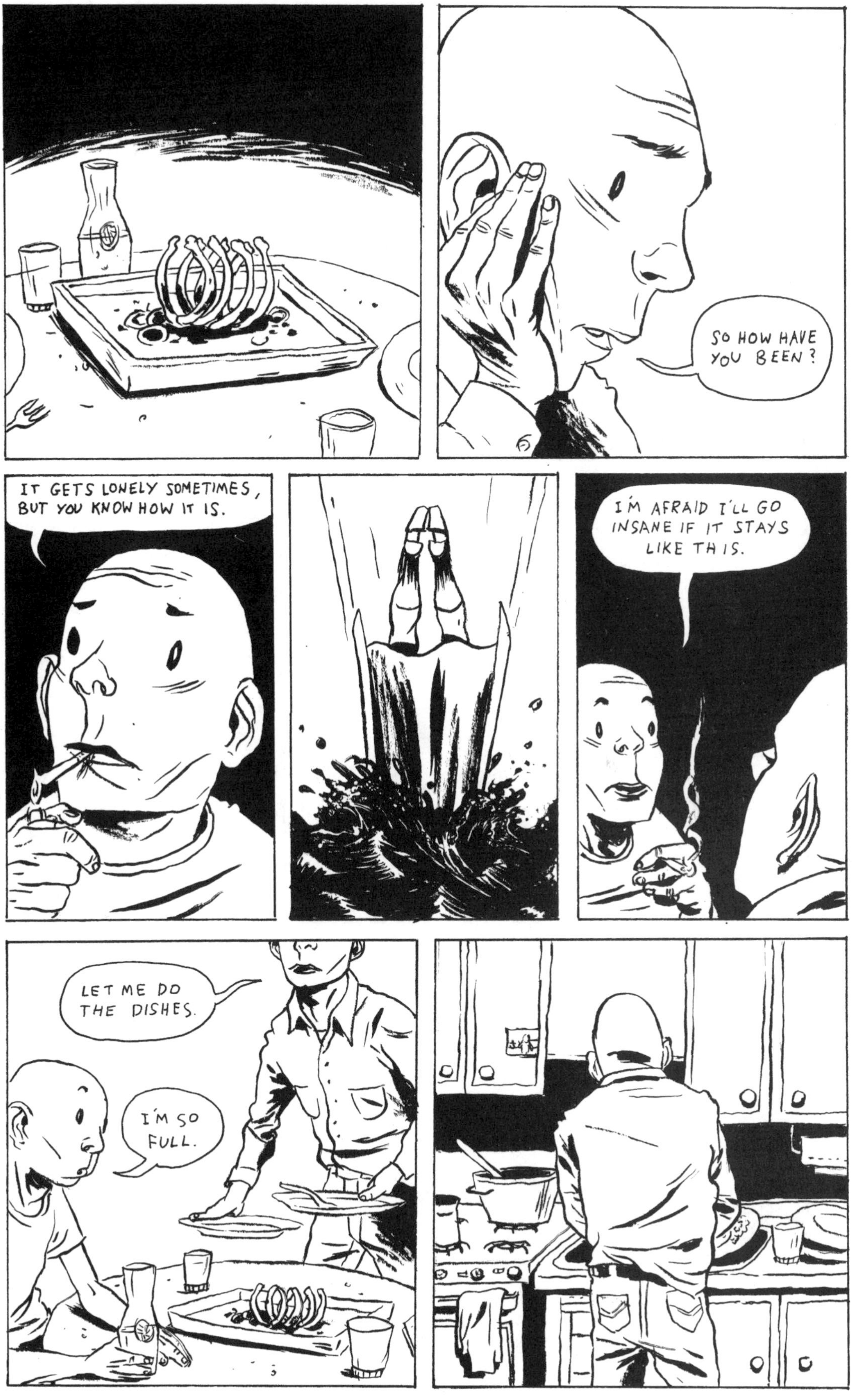
SO HOW HAVE YOU BEEN?
IT GETS LONELY SOMETIMES, BUT YOU KNOW HOW IT IS.
I'M AFRAID I'LL GO INSANE IF IT STAYS LIKE THIS.
LET ME DO THE DISHES.
I'M SO FULL.

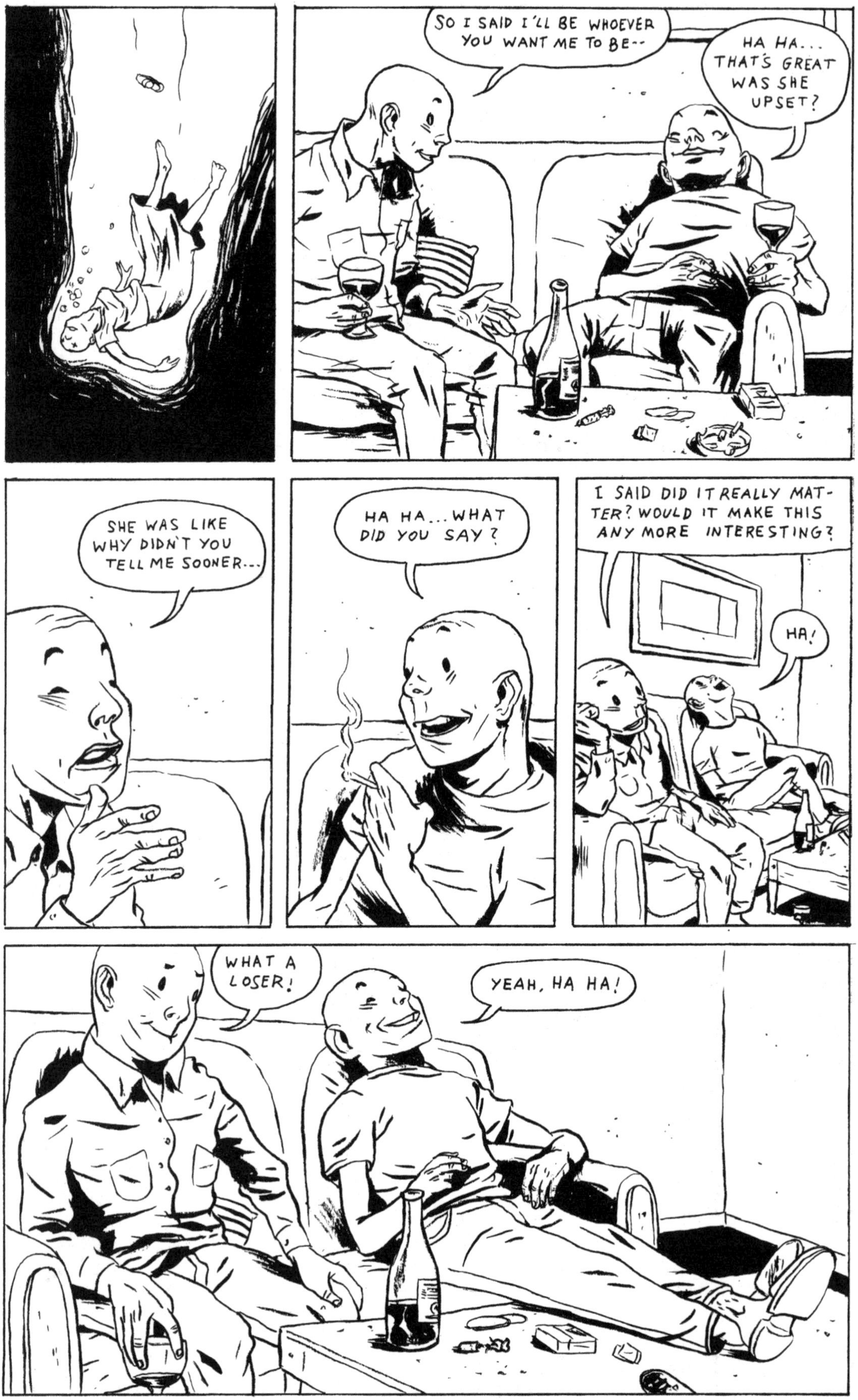
SO I SAID I'LL BE WHOEVER YOU WANT ME TO BE--
HA HA... THAT'S GREAT WAS SHE UPSET?
SHE WAS LIKE WHY DIDN'T YOU TELL ME SOONER...
HA HA... WHAT DID YOU SAY?
I SAID DID IT REALLY MATTER? WOULD IT MAKE THIS ANY MORE INTERESTING?
HA!
WHAT A LOSER!
YEAH, HA HA!

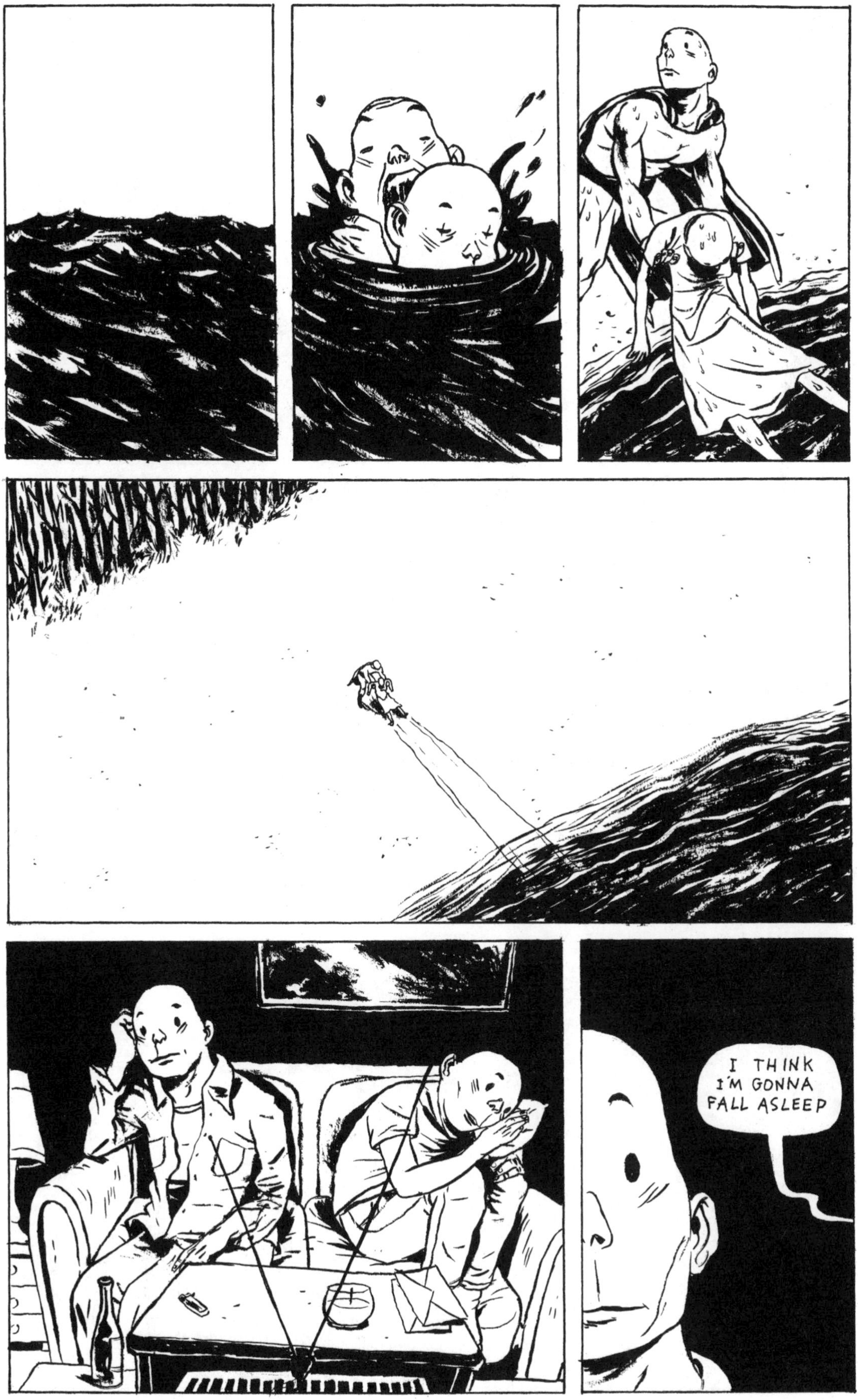
I THINK I'M GONNA FALL ASLEEP

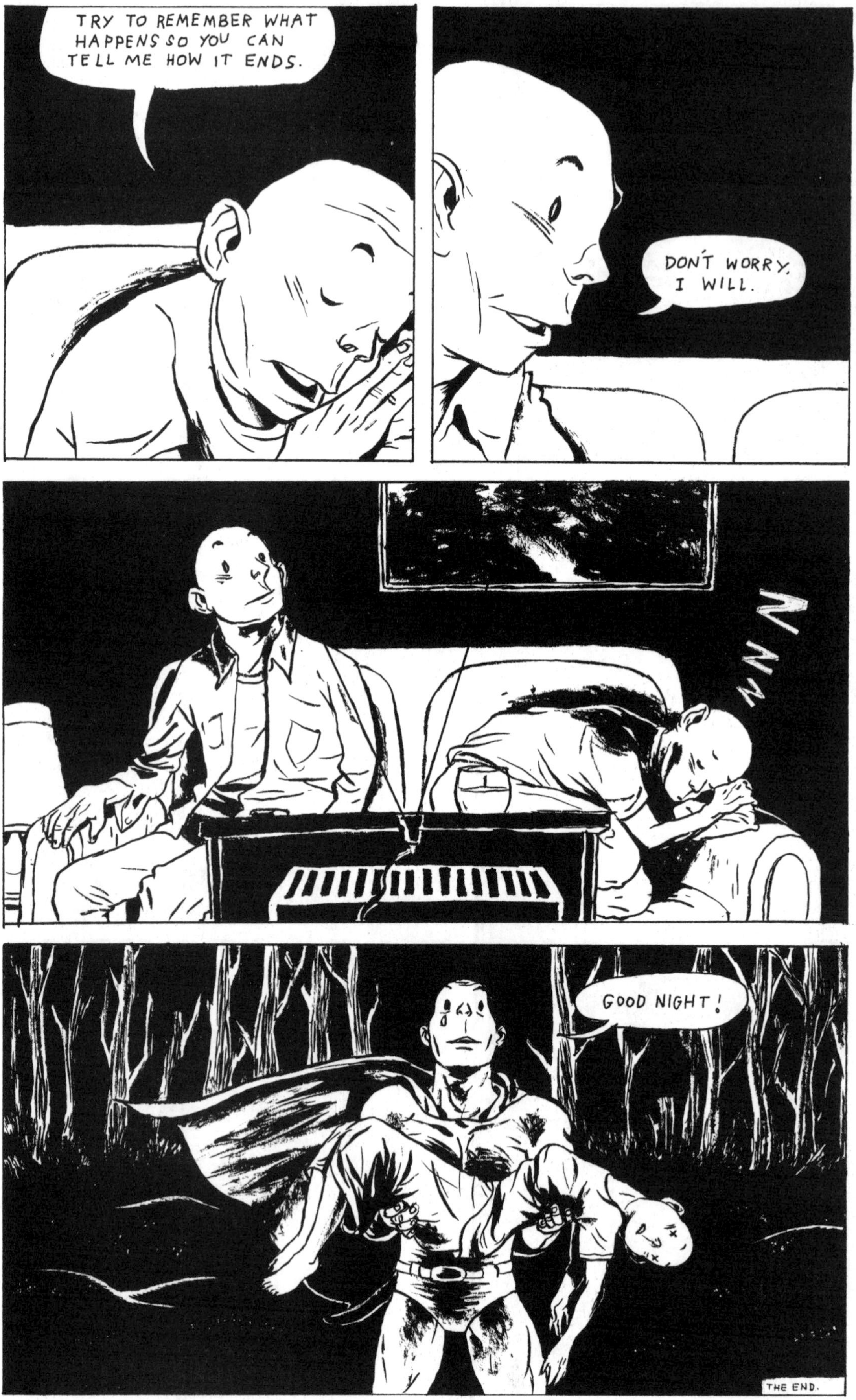

TRY TO REMEMBER WHAT HAPPENS SO YOU CAN TELL ME HOW IT ENDS.
DON'T WORRY. I WILL.
NNN
GOOD NIGHT!
THE END.

Elephant Graveyard

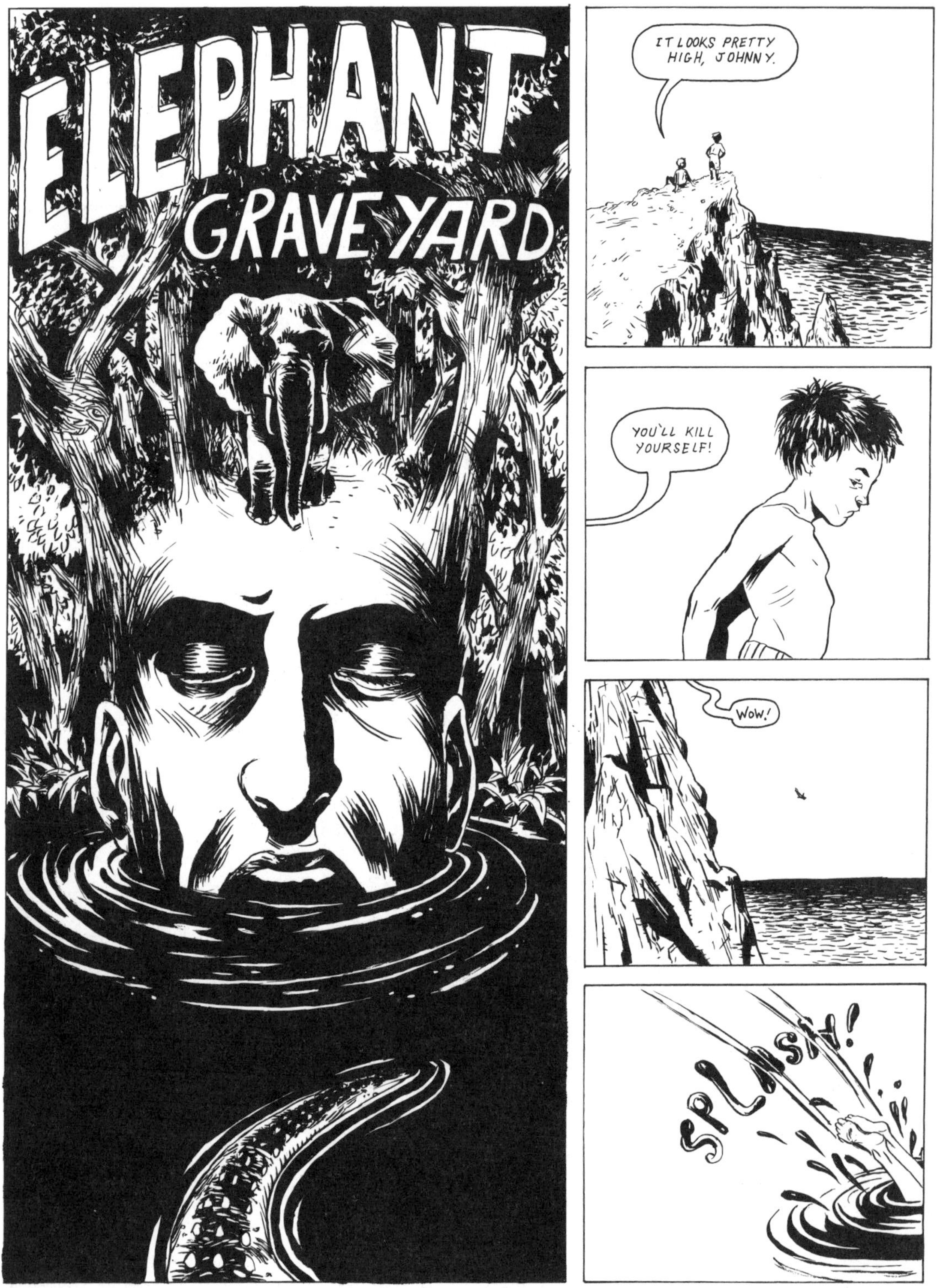
ELEPHANT
GRAVEYARD
IT LOOKS PRETTY HIGH, JOHNNY.
YOU'LL KILL YOURSELF!
WOW!
SPLASH!

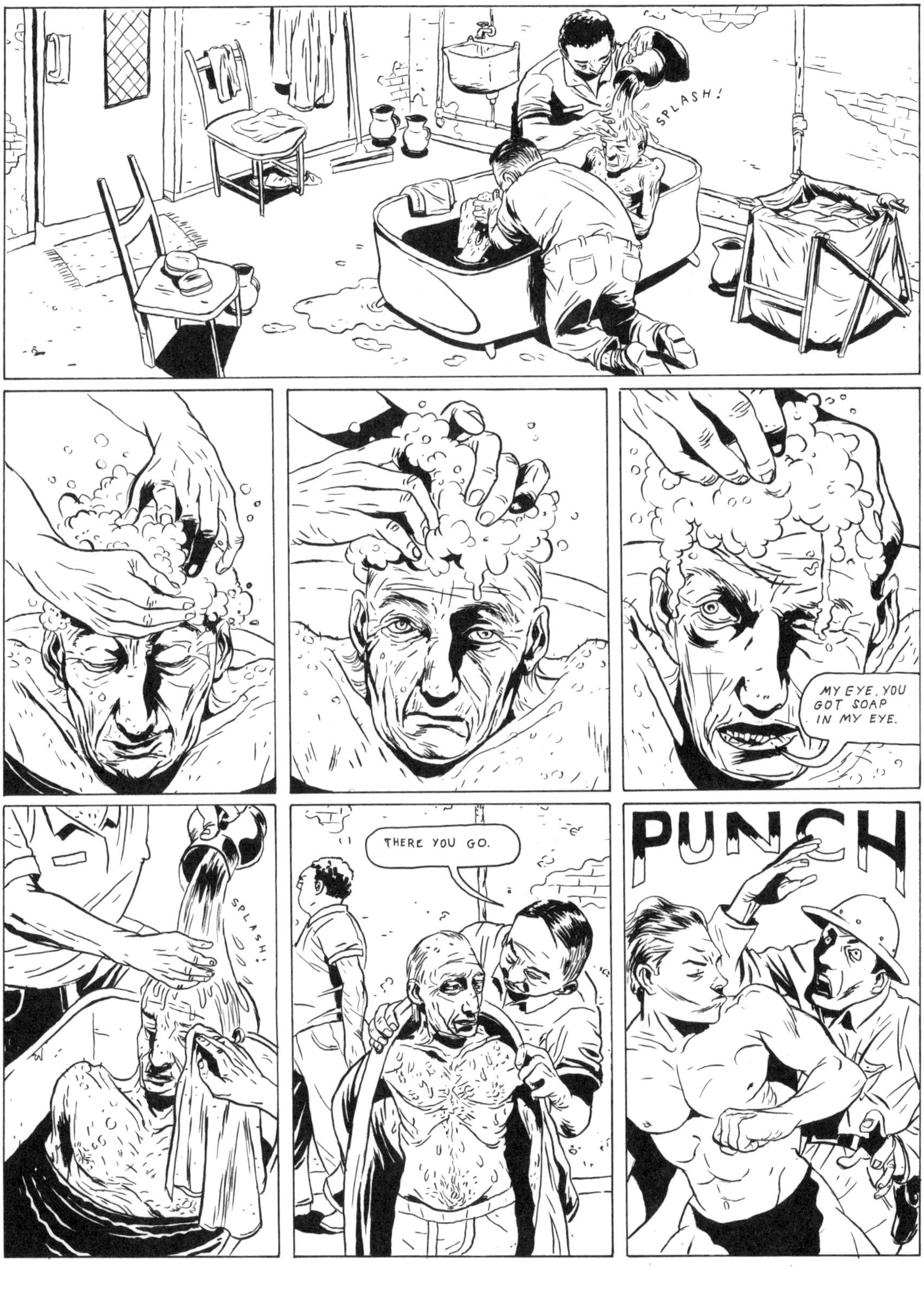
SPLASH!
MY EYE. YOU GOT SOAP IN MY EYE.
SPLASH!
THERE YOU GO.
PUNCH

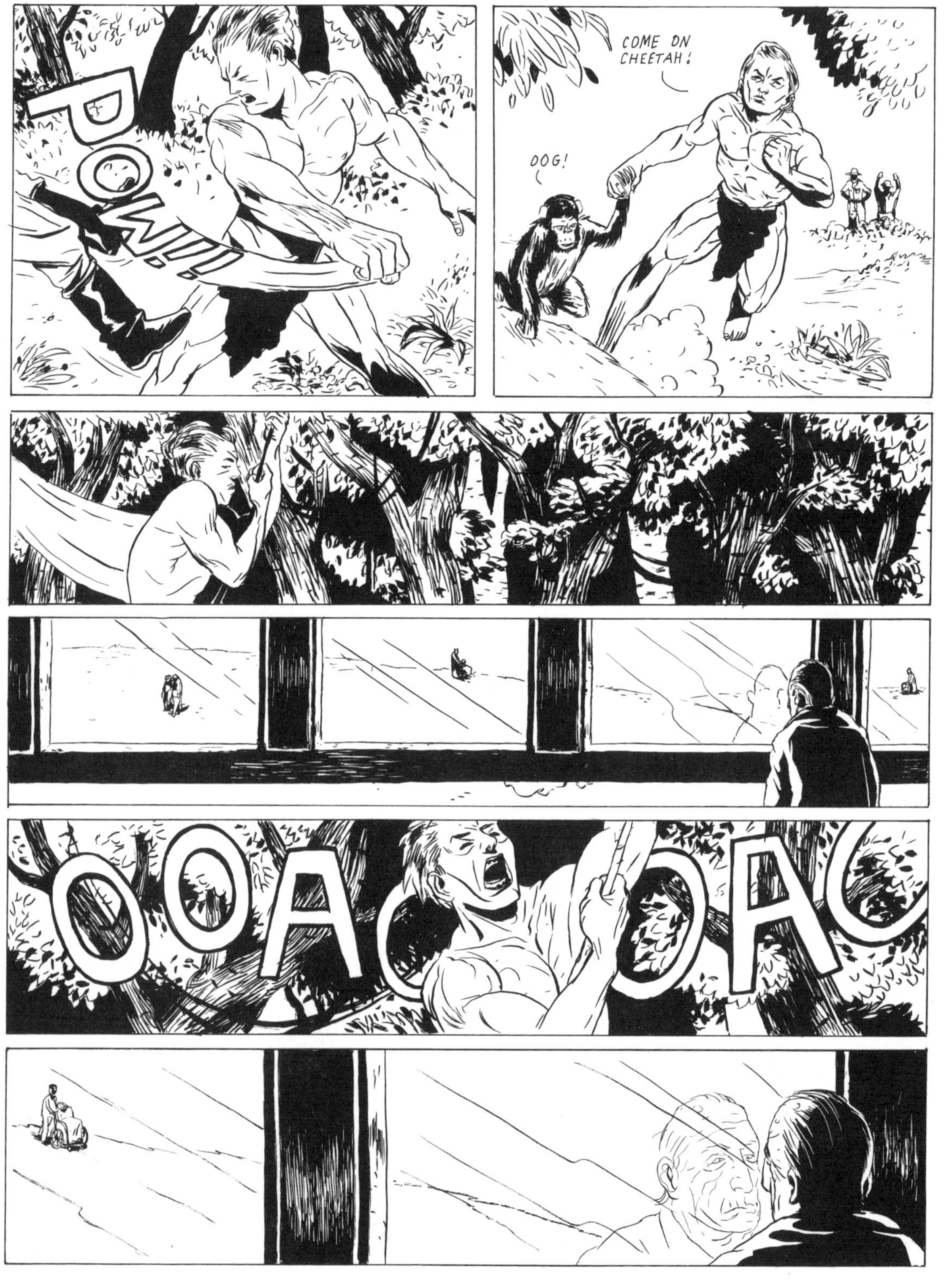
POW!!
COME ON CHEETAH!
OOG!
OOAOOAO

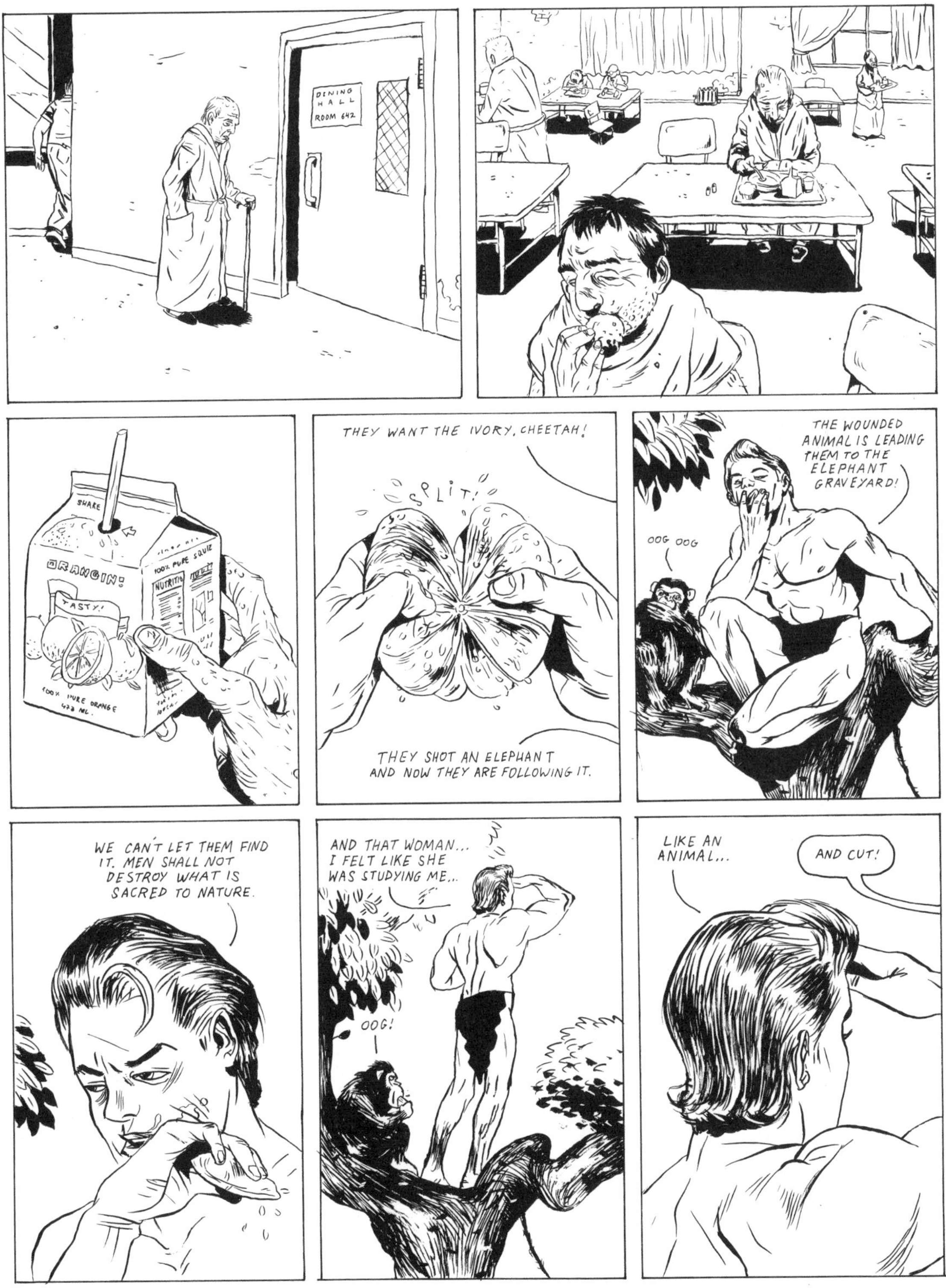
DINING HALL ROOM 642
SHARE
ORANGIN!
100% PURE SQUIZ
TASTY!
100% PURE ORANGE 473 ML.
THEY WANT THE IVORY, CHEETAH!
SPLIT!
THEY SHOT AN ELEPHANT AND NOW THEY ARE FOLLOWING IT.
THE WOUNDED ANIMAL IS LEADING THEM TO THE ELEPHANT GRAVEYARD!
OOG OOG
WE CAN'T LET THEM FIND IT. MEN SHALL NOT DESTROY WHAT IS SACRED TO NATURE.
AND THAT WOMAN... I FELT LIKE SHE WAS STUDYING ME...
OOG!
LIKE AN ANIMAL...
AND CUT!

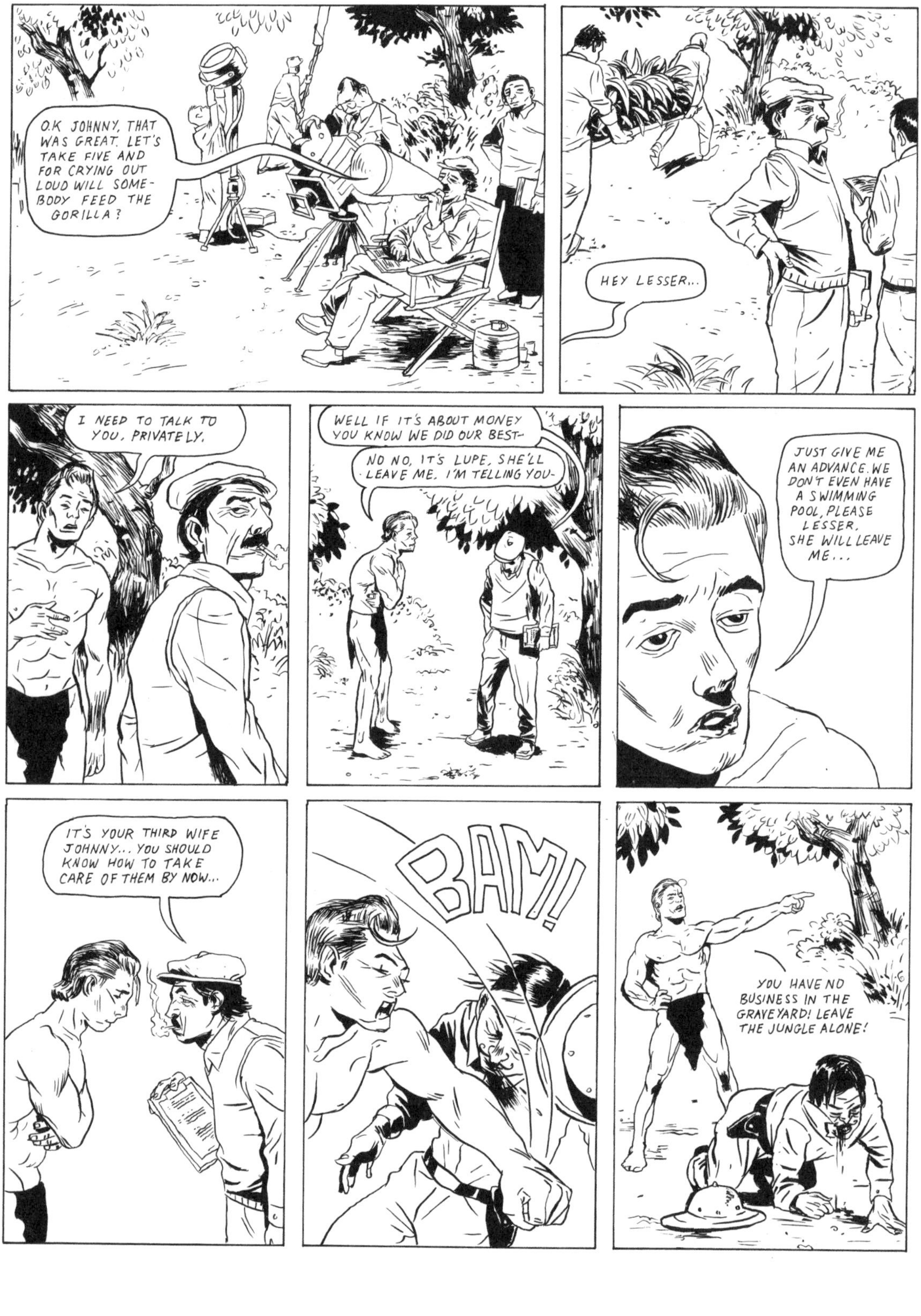
O.K JOHNNY, THAT WAS GREAT. LET'S TAKE FIVE AND FOR CRYING OUT LOUD WILL SOMEBODY FEED THE GORILLA?
HEY LESSER...
I NEED TO TALK TO YOU, PRIVATELY.
WELL IF IT'S ABOUT MONEY YOU KNOW WE DID OUR BEST-
NO NO, IT'S LUPE, SHE'LL LEAVE ME. I'M TELLING YOU-
JUST GIVE ME AN ADVANCE. WE DON'T EVEN HAVE A SWIMMING POOL, PLEASE LESSER. SHE WILL LEAVE ME...
IT'S YOUR THIRD WIFE JOHNNY... YOU SHOULD KNOW HOW TO TAKE CARE OF THEM BY NOW...
BAM!
YOU HAVE NO BUSINESS IN THE GRAVEYARD! LEAVE THE JUNGLE ALONE!

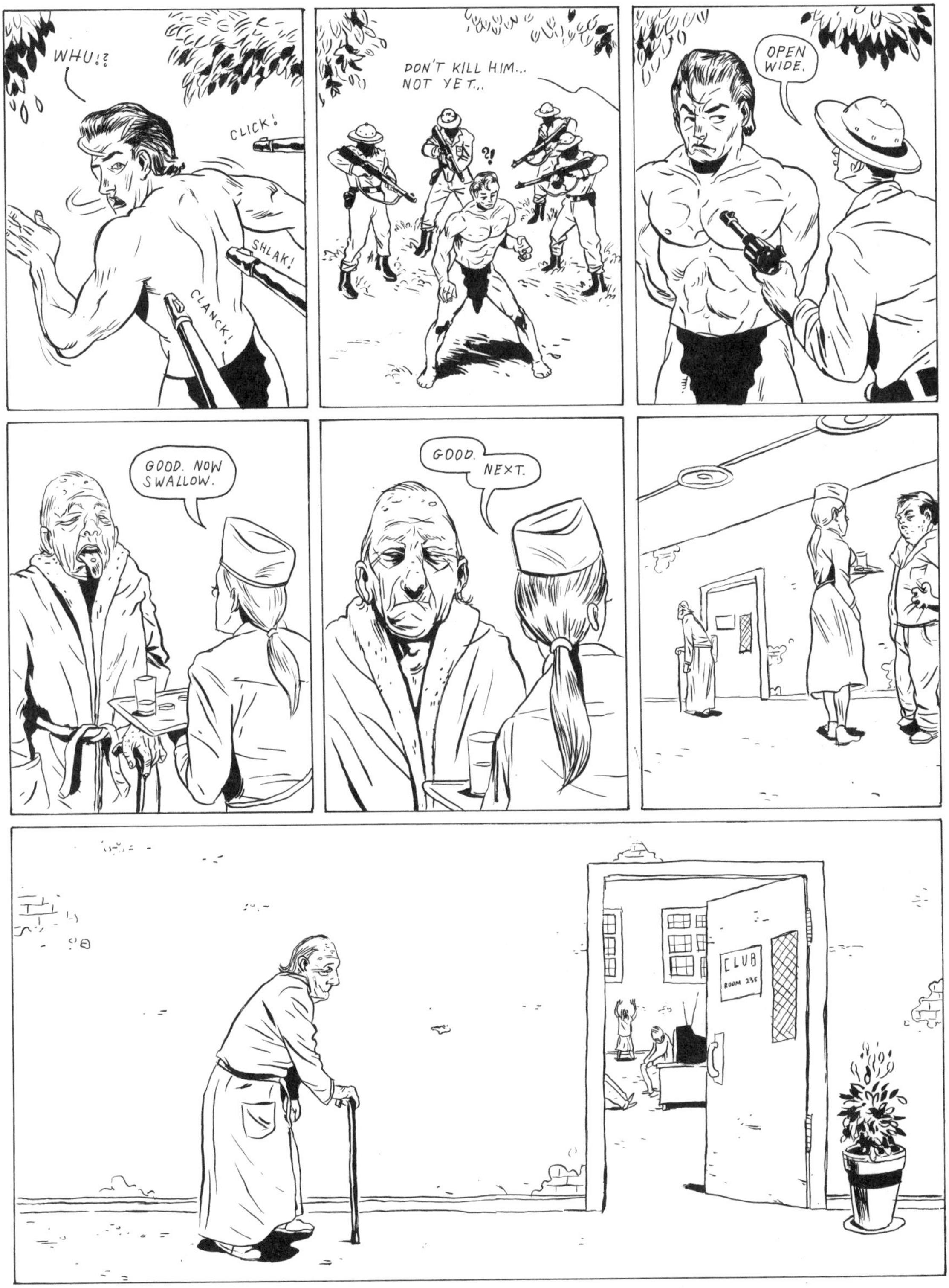
WHU!?
CLICK!
SHLAK!
CLANCK!
DON'T KILL HIM... NOT YET...
?!
OPEN WIDE.
GOOD. NOW SWALLOW.
GOOD.
NEXT.
CLUB
ROOM 235

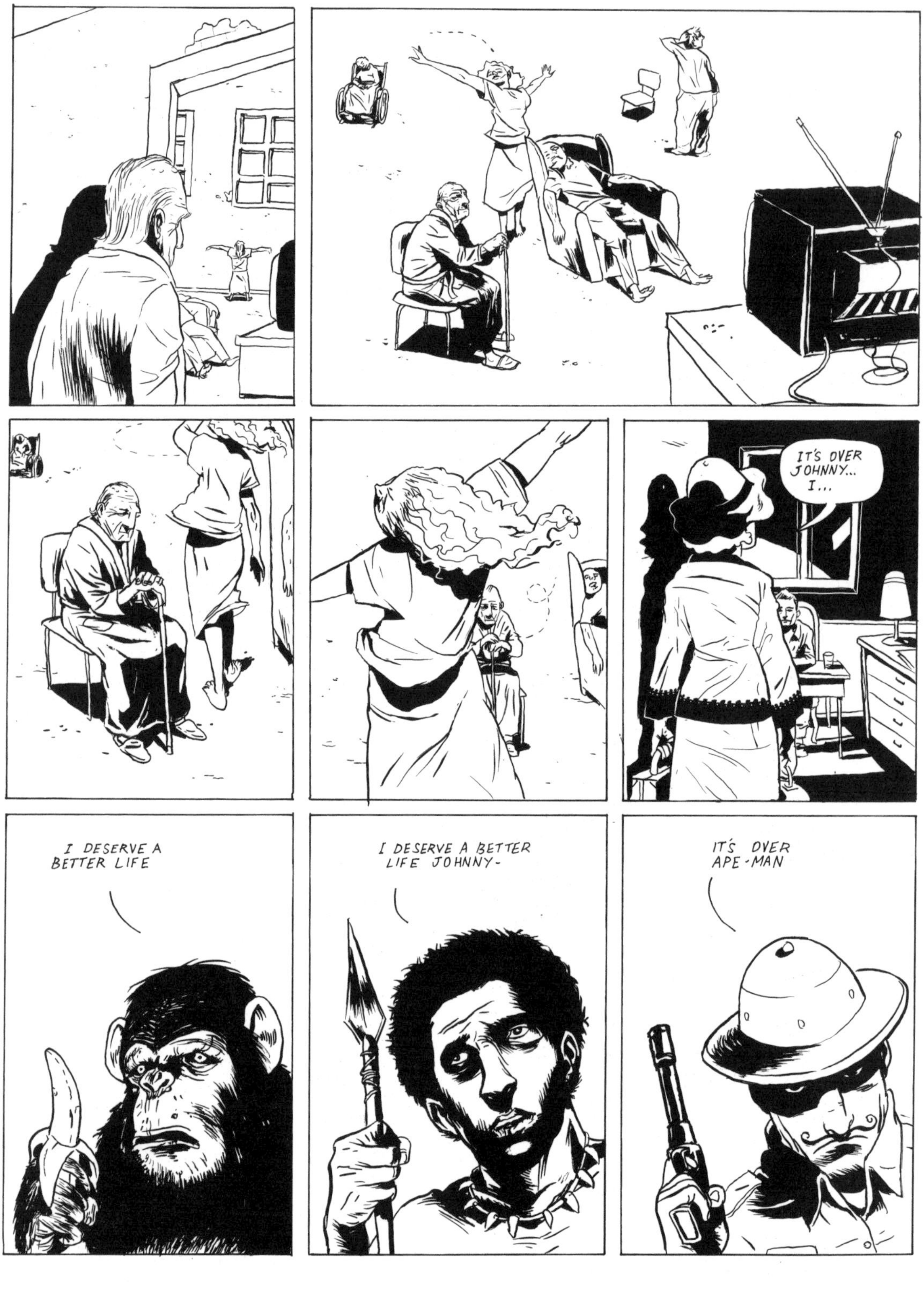
IT'S OVER JOHNNY... I...
I DESERVE A BETTER LIFE
I DESERVE A BETTER LIFE JOHNNY-
IT'S OVER APE-MAN

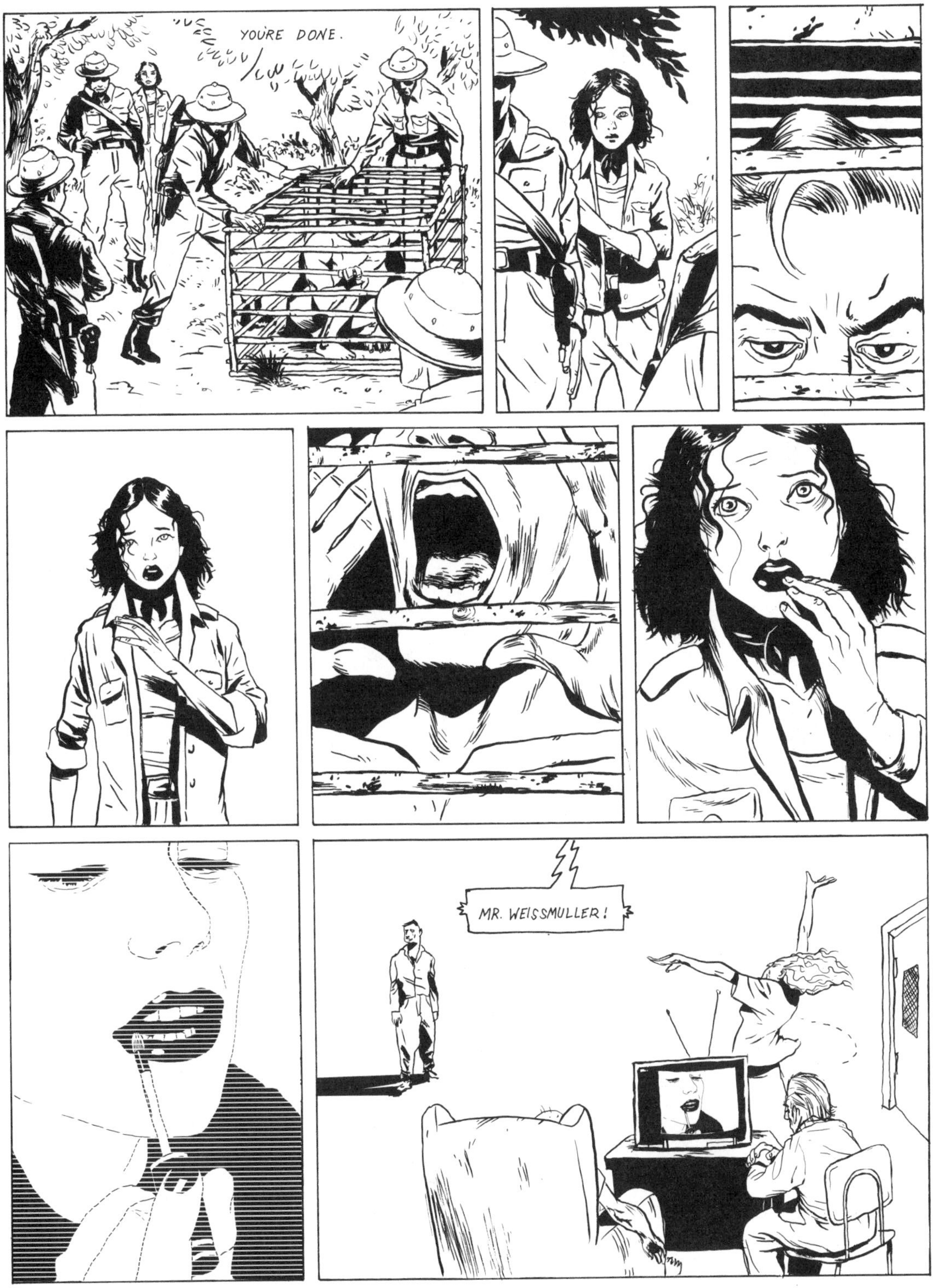
YOU'RE DONE.
MR. WEISSMULLER!

MR. WEISSMULLER, DAILY CHECK UP, PLEASE GO TO ROOM 436.
ROOM 436 - CLINIC
HEY THERE MR. WEISSMULLER, PLEASE COME IN.
LET'S SEE NOW...
HMM...
HMF...

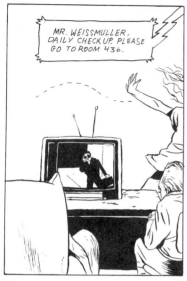

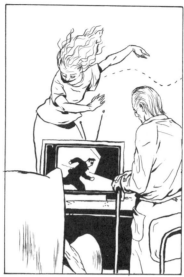

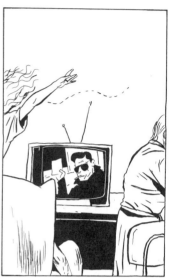

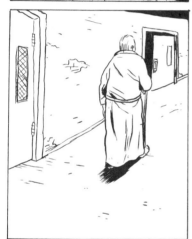

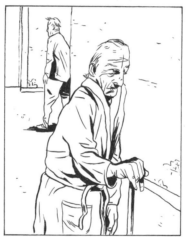

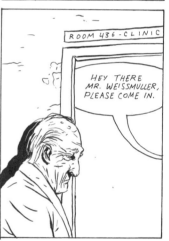

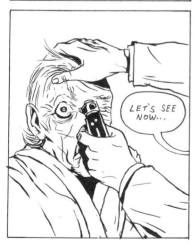

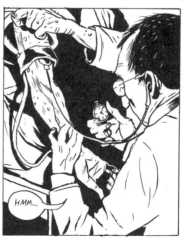

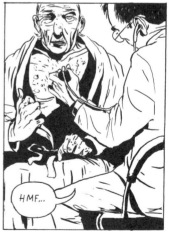

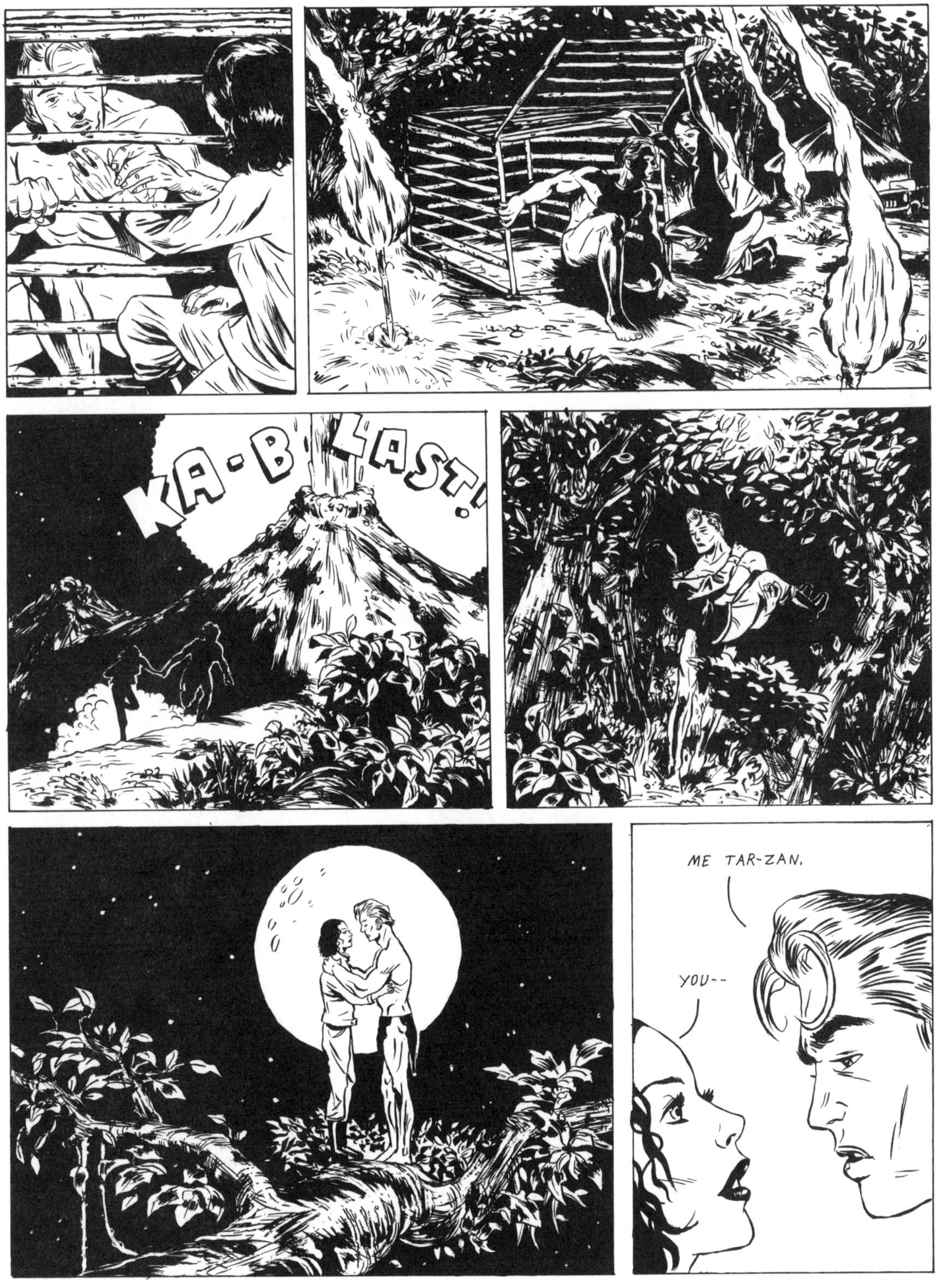
KA-BLAST!
ME TAR-ZAN.
YOU--

YOUR HEART IS GOOD.

BLOOD PRESSURE SEEMS A LITTLE OFF THOUGH, BUT THAT'S NOT UNUSUAL AT YOUR AGE...

I WILL SEE YOU TOMORROW, HAVE A GOOD DAY NOW.

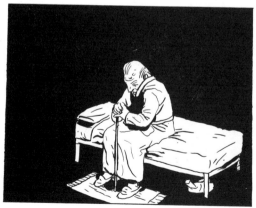

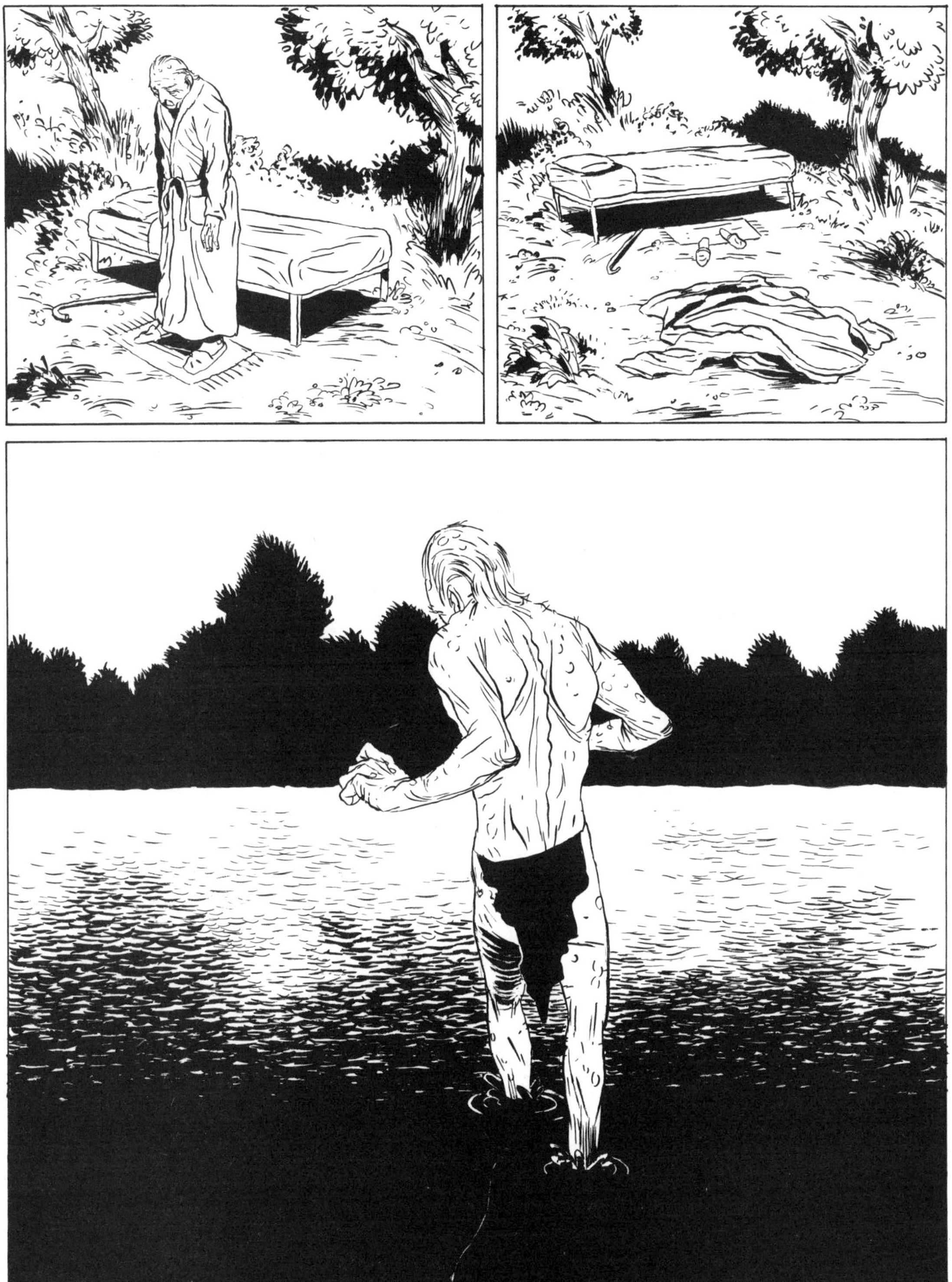

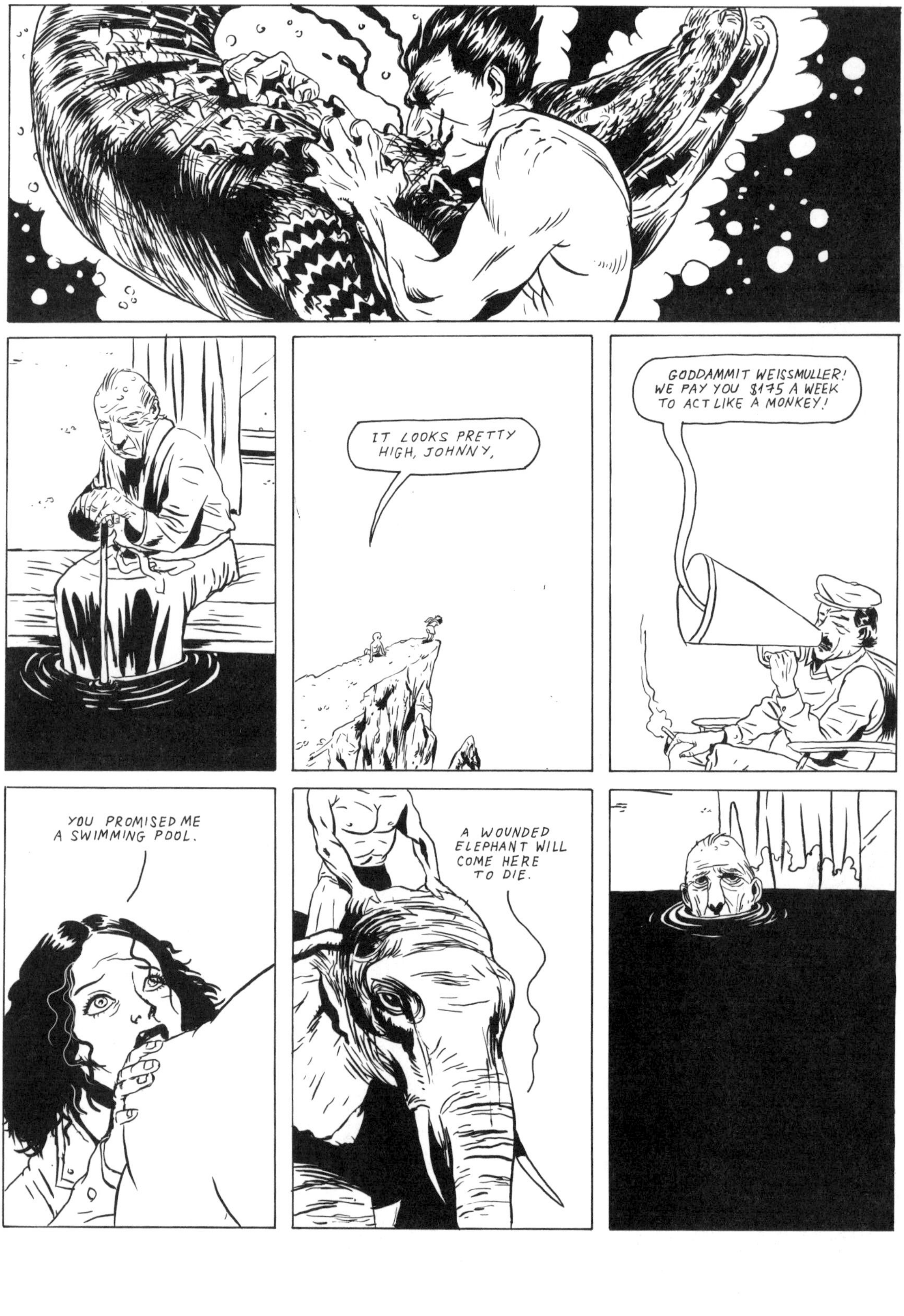
IT LOOKS PRETTY HIGH, JOHNNY,
GODDAMMIT WEISSMULLER! WE PAY YOU $175 A WEEK TO ACT LIKE A MONKEY!
YOU PROMISED ME A SWIMMING POOL.
A WOUNDED ELEPHANT WILL COME HERE TO DIE.

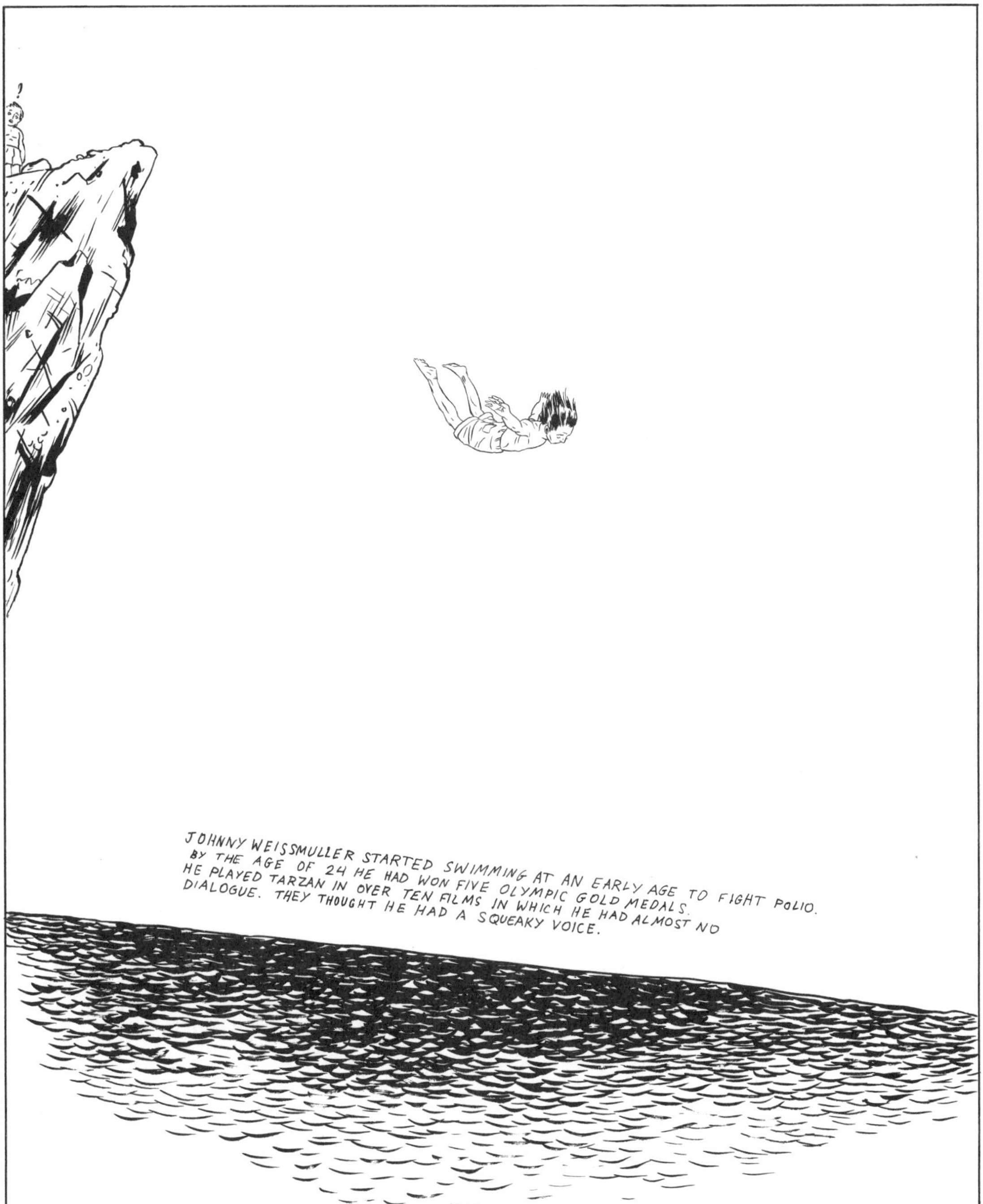
?
JOHNNY WEISSMULLER STARTED SWIMMING AT AN EARLY AGE TO FIGHT POLIO.
BY THE AGE OF 24 HE HAD WON FIVE OLYMPIC GOLD MEDALS.
HE PLAYED TARZAN IN OVER TEN FILMS IN WHICH HE HAD ALMOST NO DIALOGUE. THEY THOUGHT HE HAD A SQUEAKY VOICE.
END.

Junior

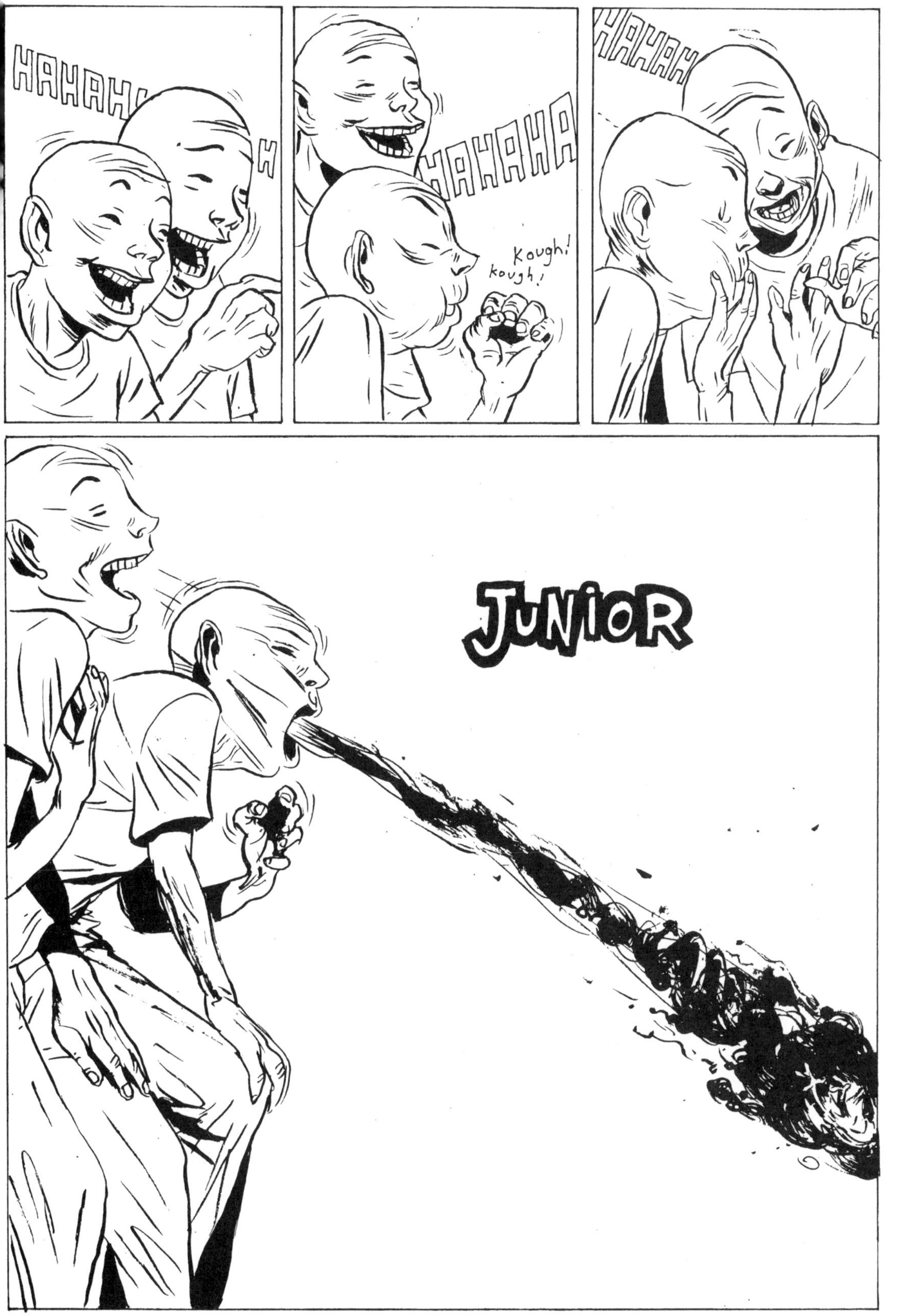
HAHAHAH
HAHAHA
Kough!
kough!
HAHAHAH
JUNIOR

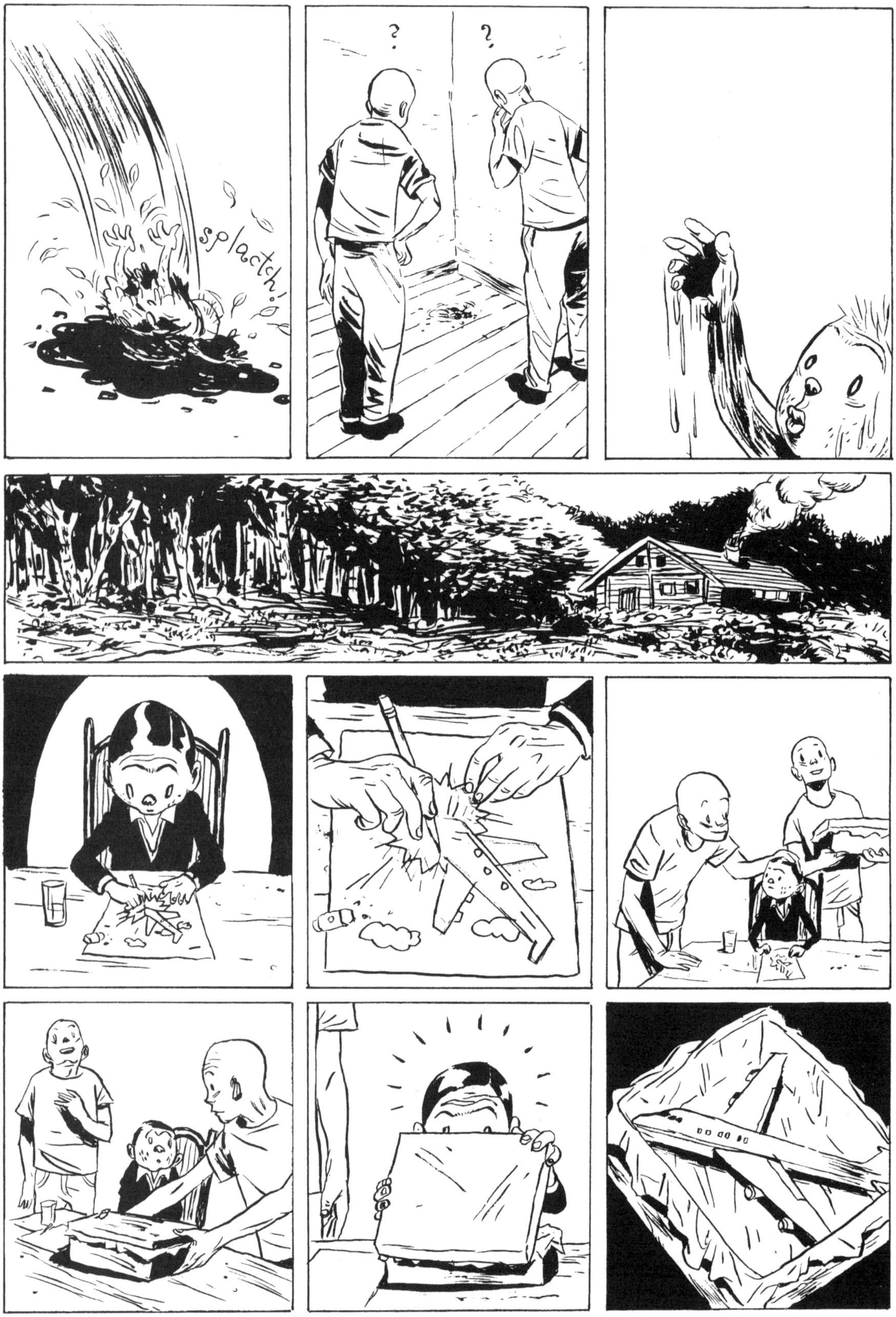
splactch!
?
?

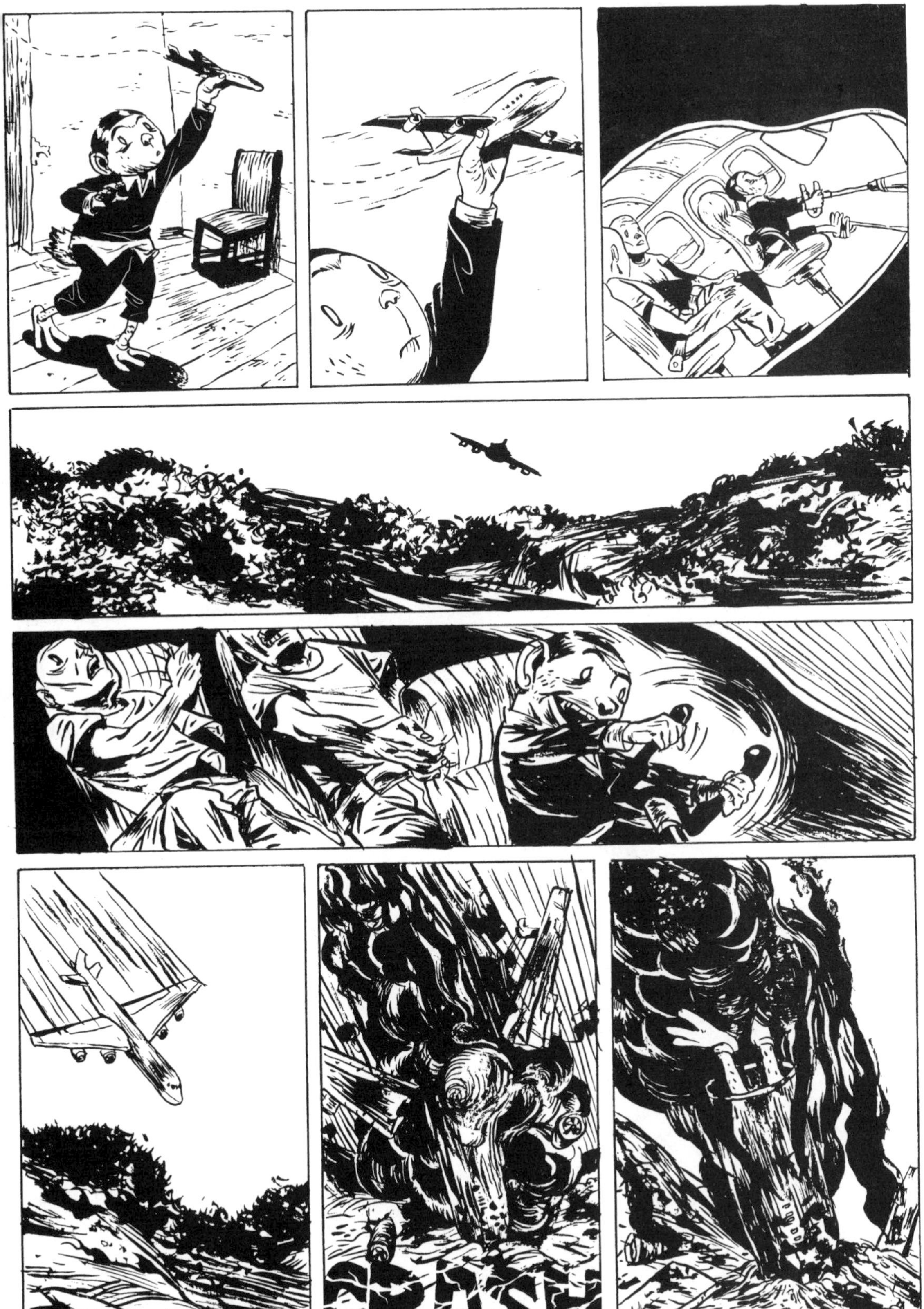
CRASH

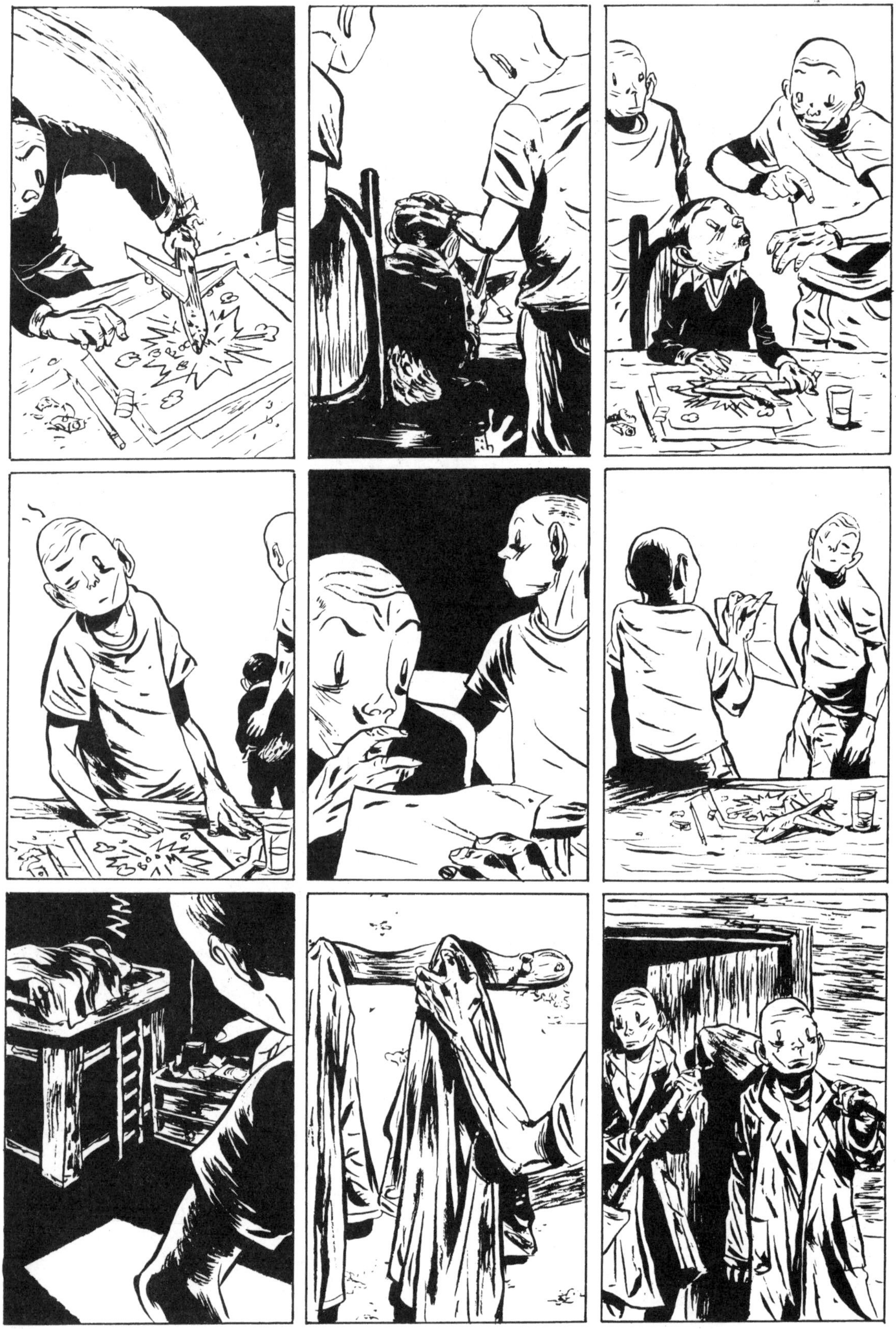

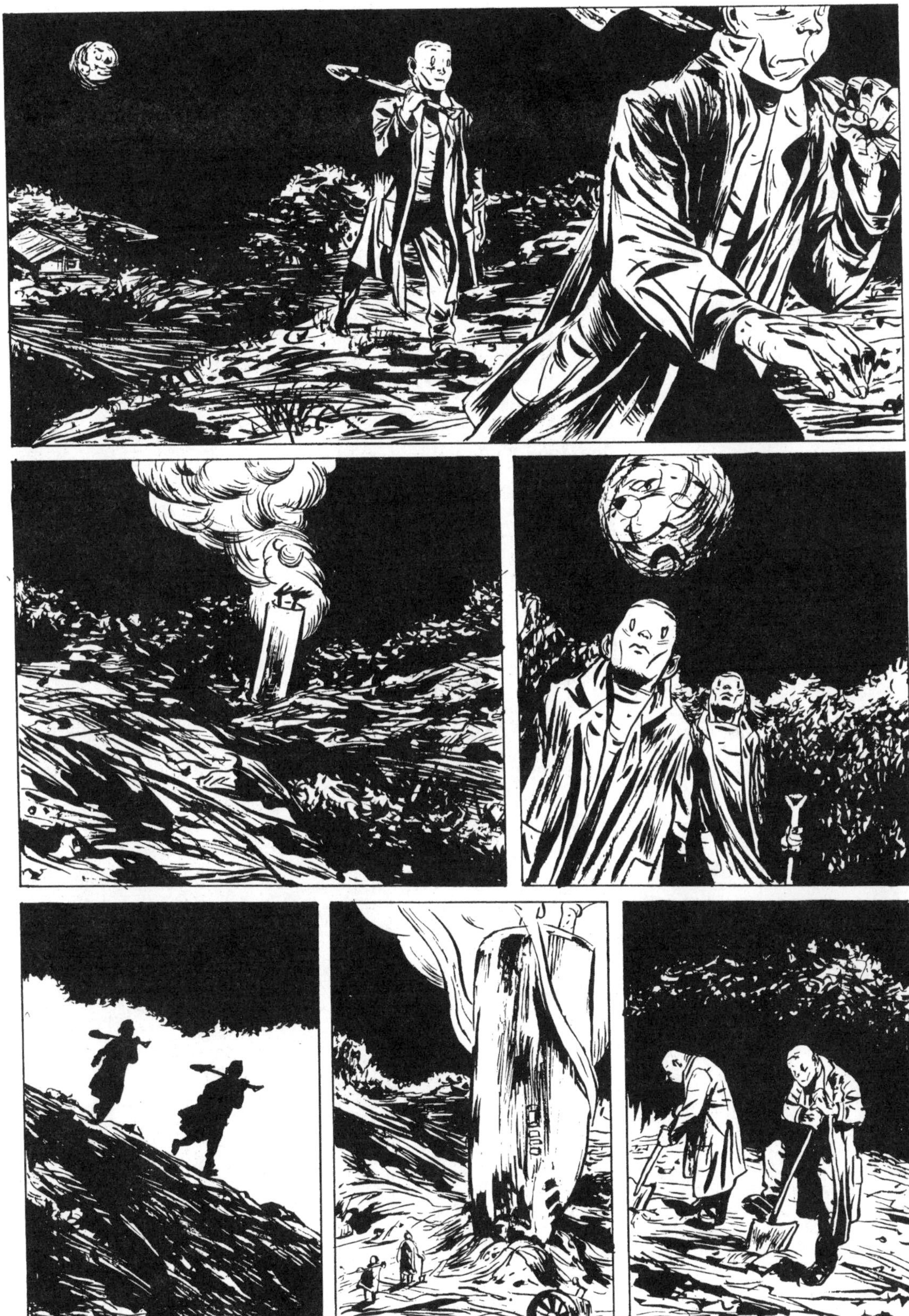

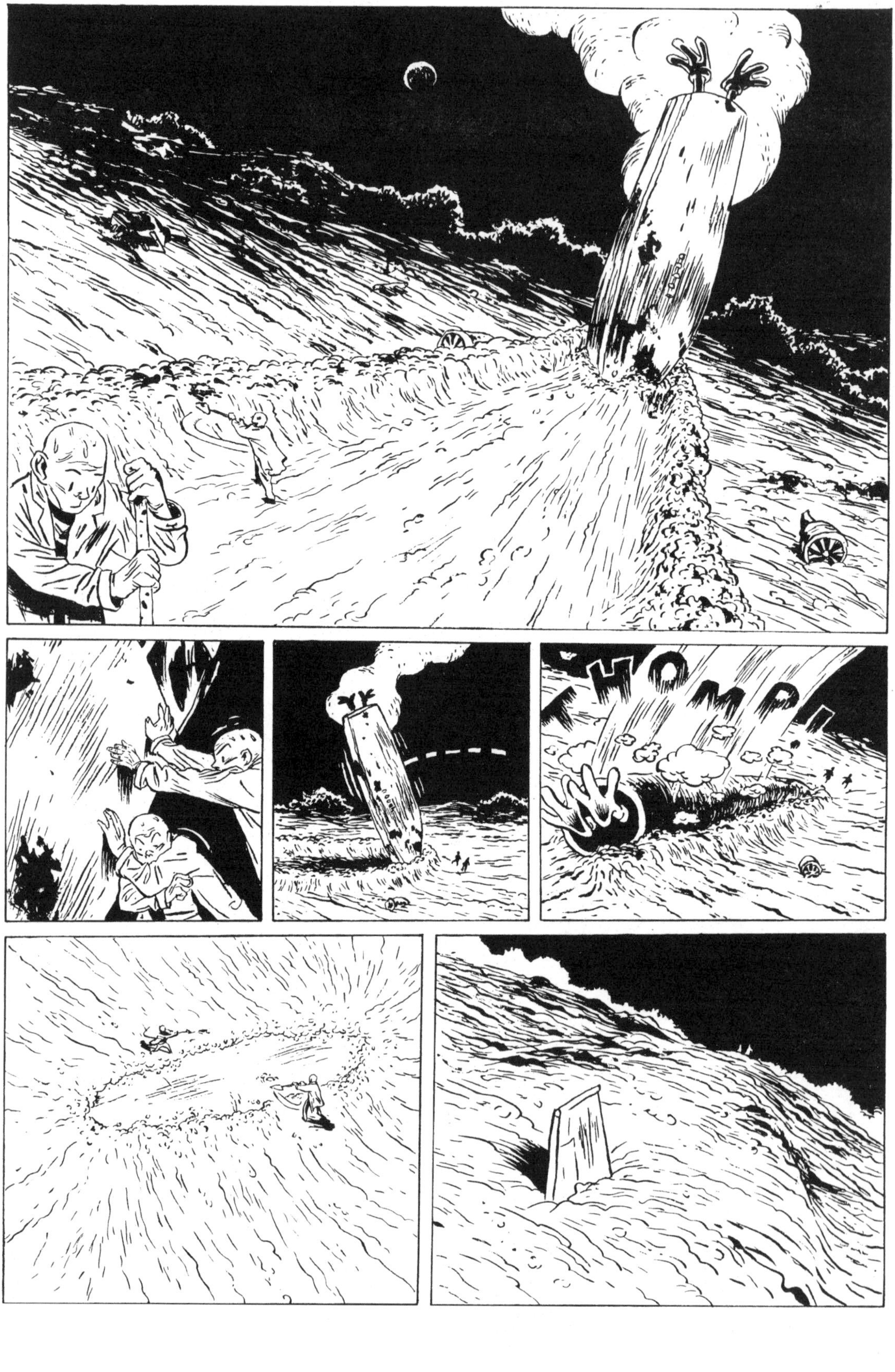
THOMP!

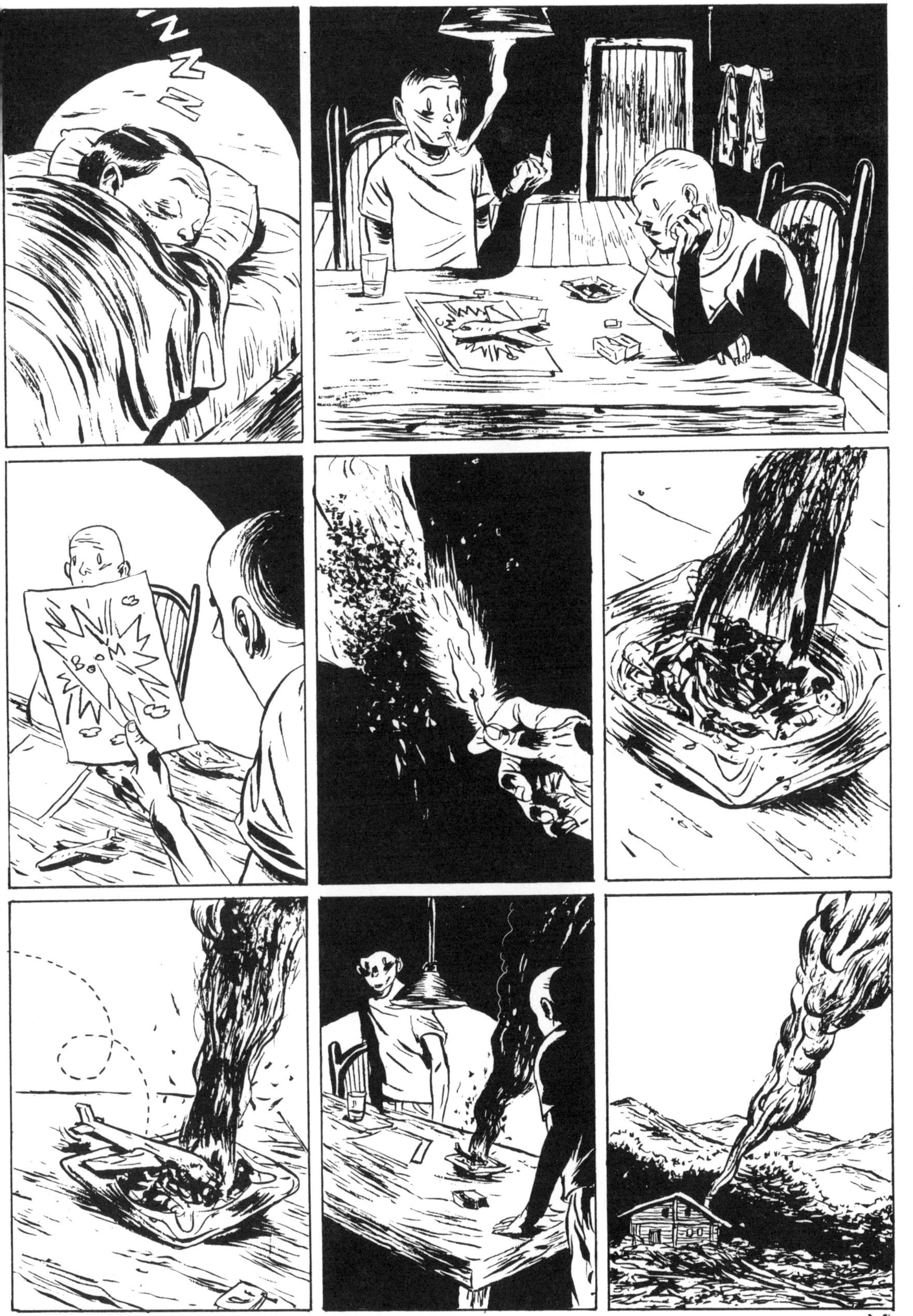
BOOM

Squeeze

SQUEEZE

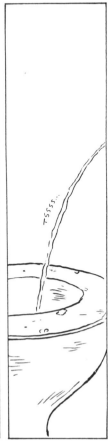

TSSSS...

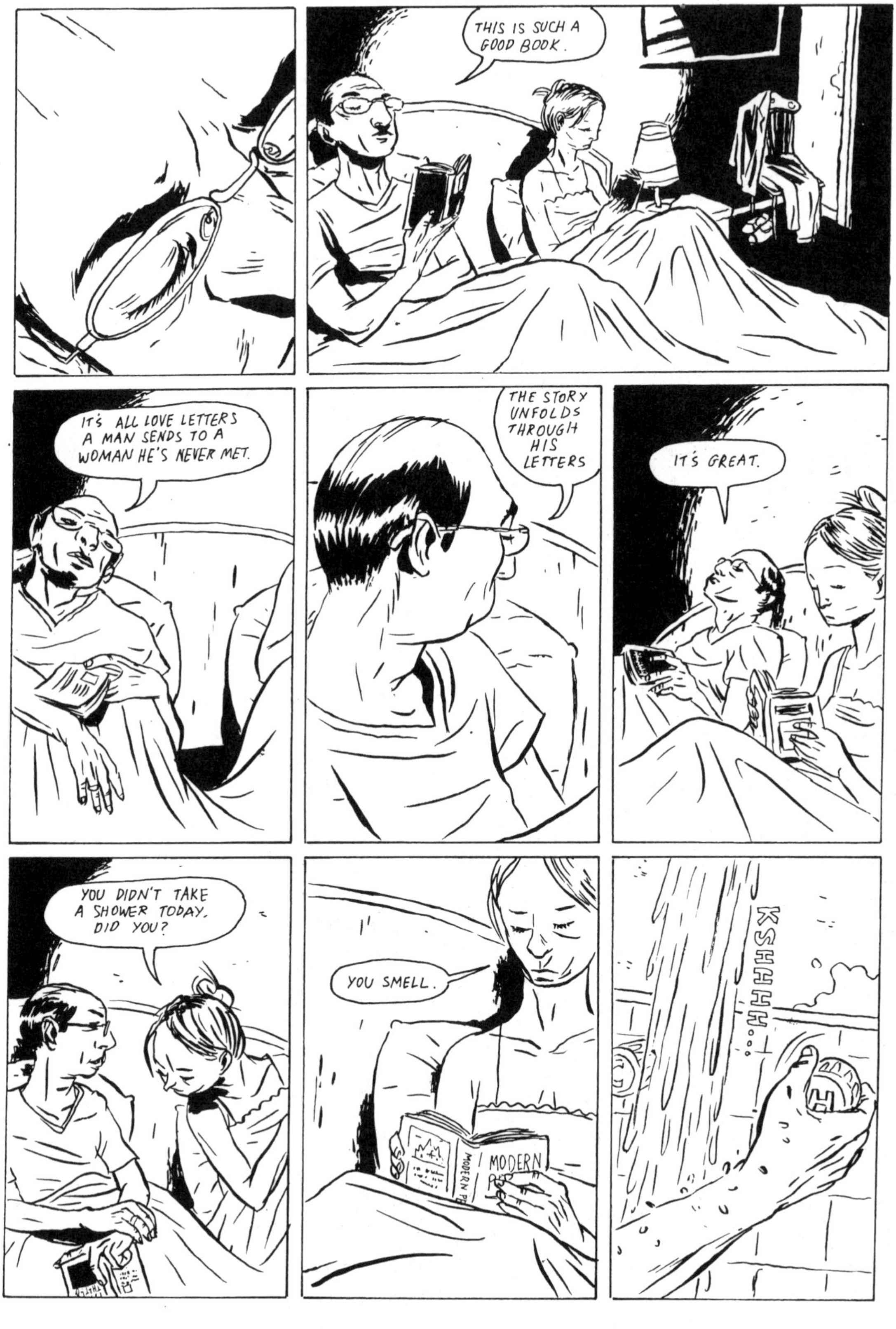
THIS IS SUCH A GOOD BOOK.
IT'S ALL LOVE LETTERS A MAN SENDS TO A WOMAN HE'S NEVER MET.
THE STORY UNFOLDS THROUGH HIS LETTERS
IT'S GREAT.
YOU DIDN'T TAKE A SHOWER TODAY, DID YOU?
YOU SMELL.
MODERN
KSHHHH...

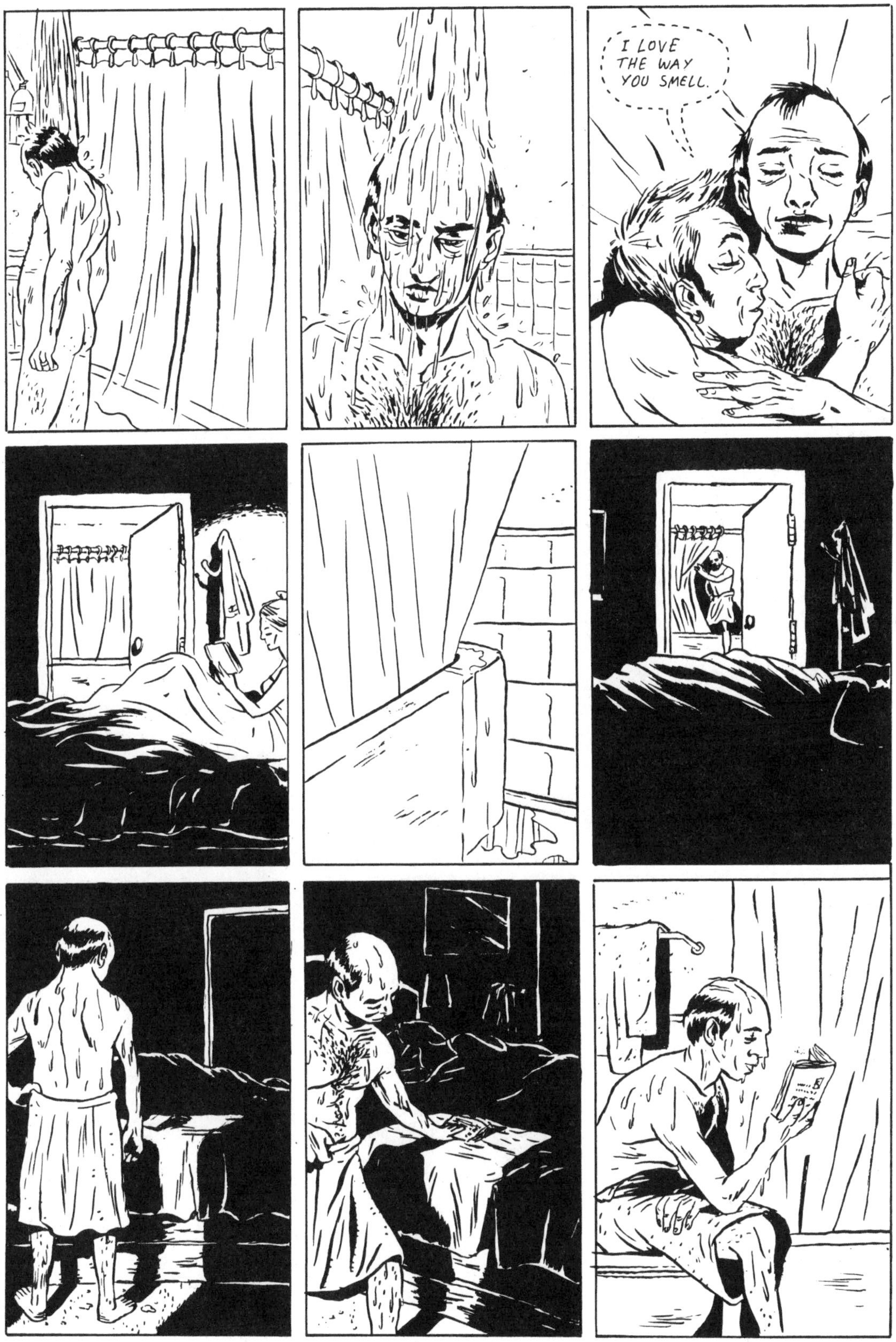
I LOVE THE WAY YOU SMELL.

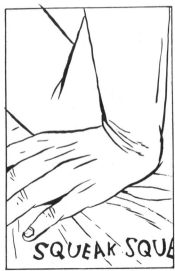

SQUEAK SQUE

SQUEAK SQUEAK SQUEAK SQUEAK SQUEAK

OH·MY·GOD!

SQUEAK SQUE--

FUCK!

JENNY! HOLD ON HOLD ON...

SOB...SOB...

HOW COULD YOU... DO THIS... TO ME..?

YOUSONOFABITCH...

JEN, THIS IS BULLSHIT, IT'S NOTHING!

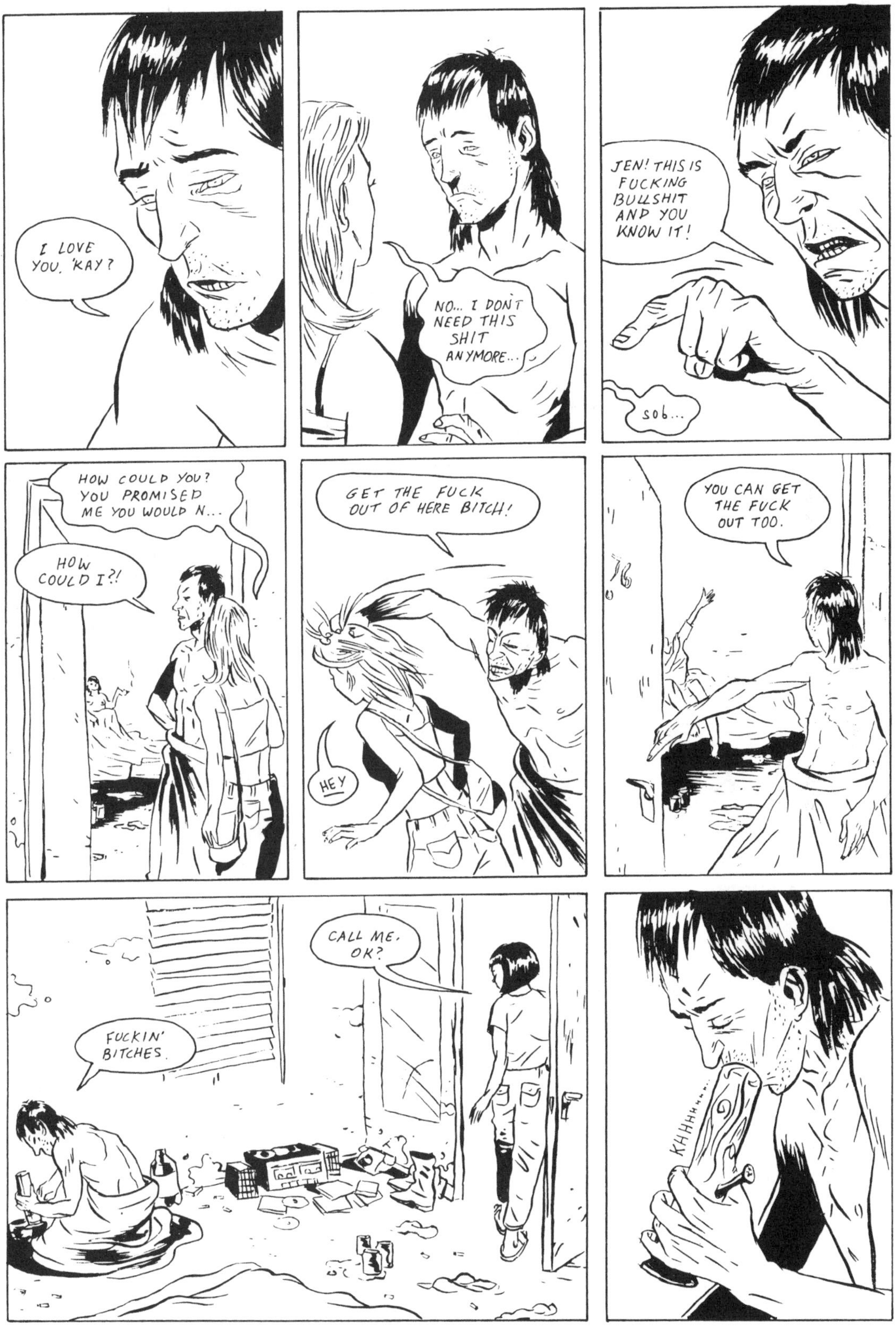
I LOVE YOU, 'KAY?
NO... I DON'T NEED THIS SHIT ANYMORE...
JEN! THIS IS FUCKING BULLSHIT AND YOU KNOW IT!
sob...
HOW COULD YOU? YOU PROMISED ME YOU WOULD N...
HOW COULD I?!
GET THE FUCK OUT OF HERE BITCH!
HEY
YOU CAN GET THE FUCK OUT TOO.
FUCKIN' BITCHES.
CALL ME, OK?
KHHHHHH...

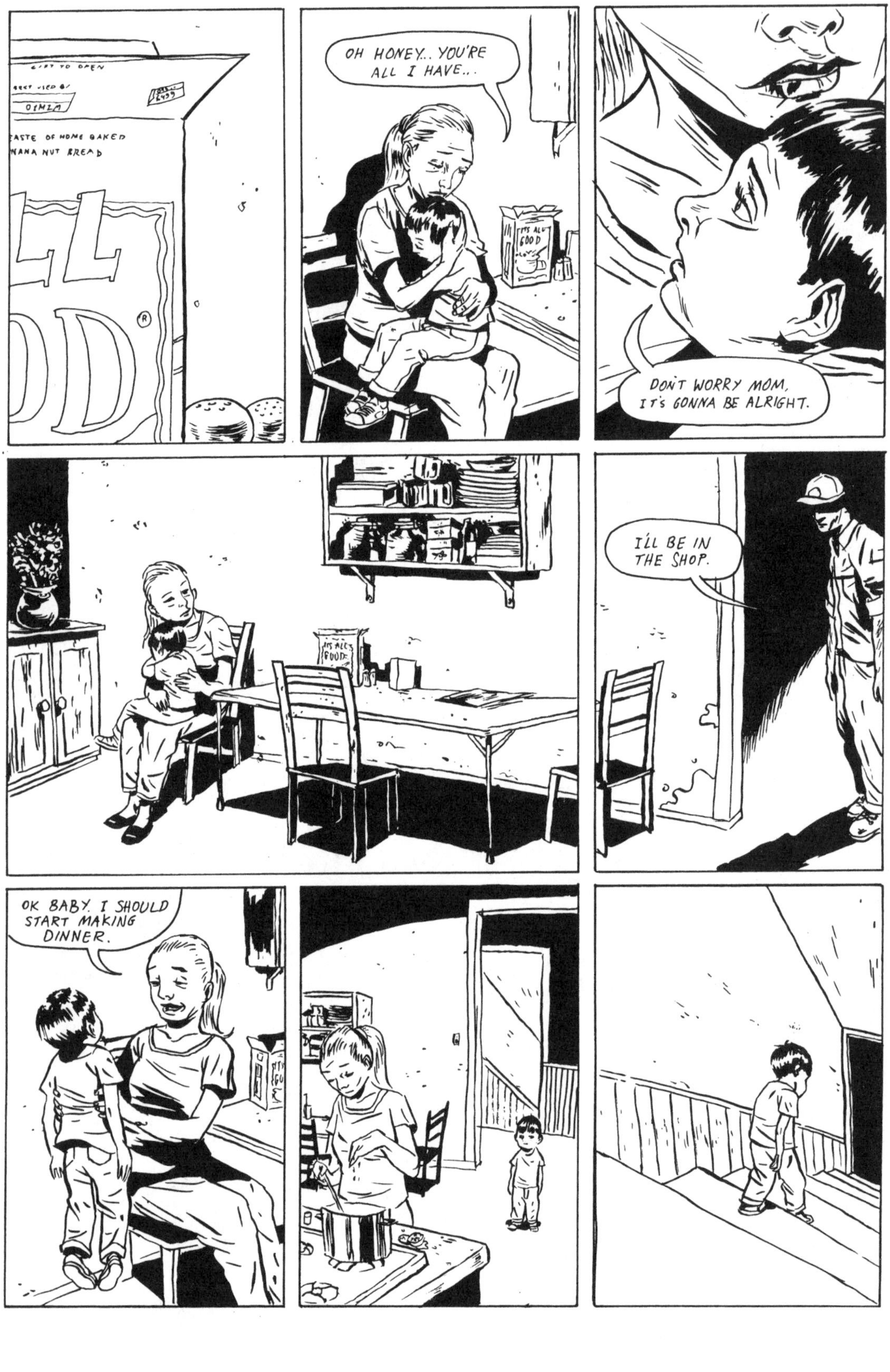
OH HONEY... YOU'RE ALL I HAVE...
DON'T WORRY MOM, IT'S GONNA BE ALRIGHT.
I'LL BE IN THE SHOP.
OK BABY. I SHOULD START MAKING DINNER.

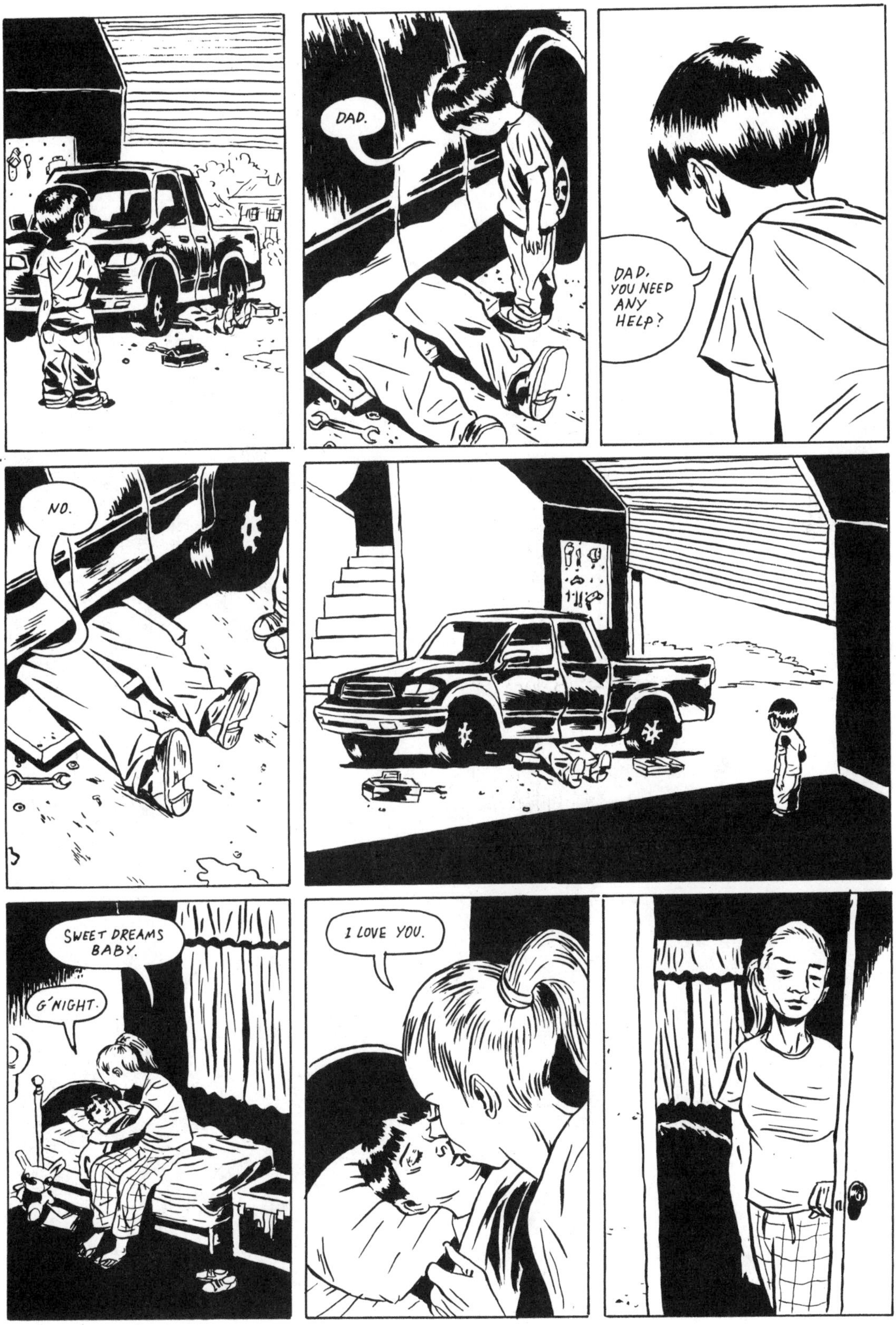
DAD.
DAD. YOU NEED ANY HELP?
NO.
SWEET DREAMS BABY.
G'NIGHT.
I LOVE YOU.

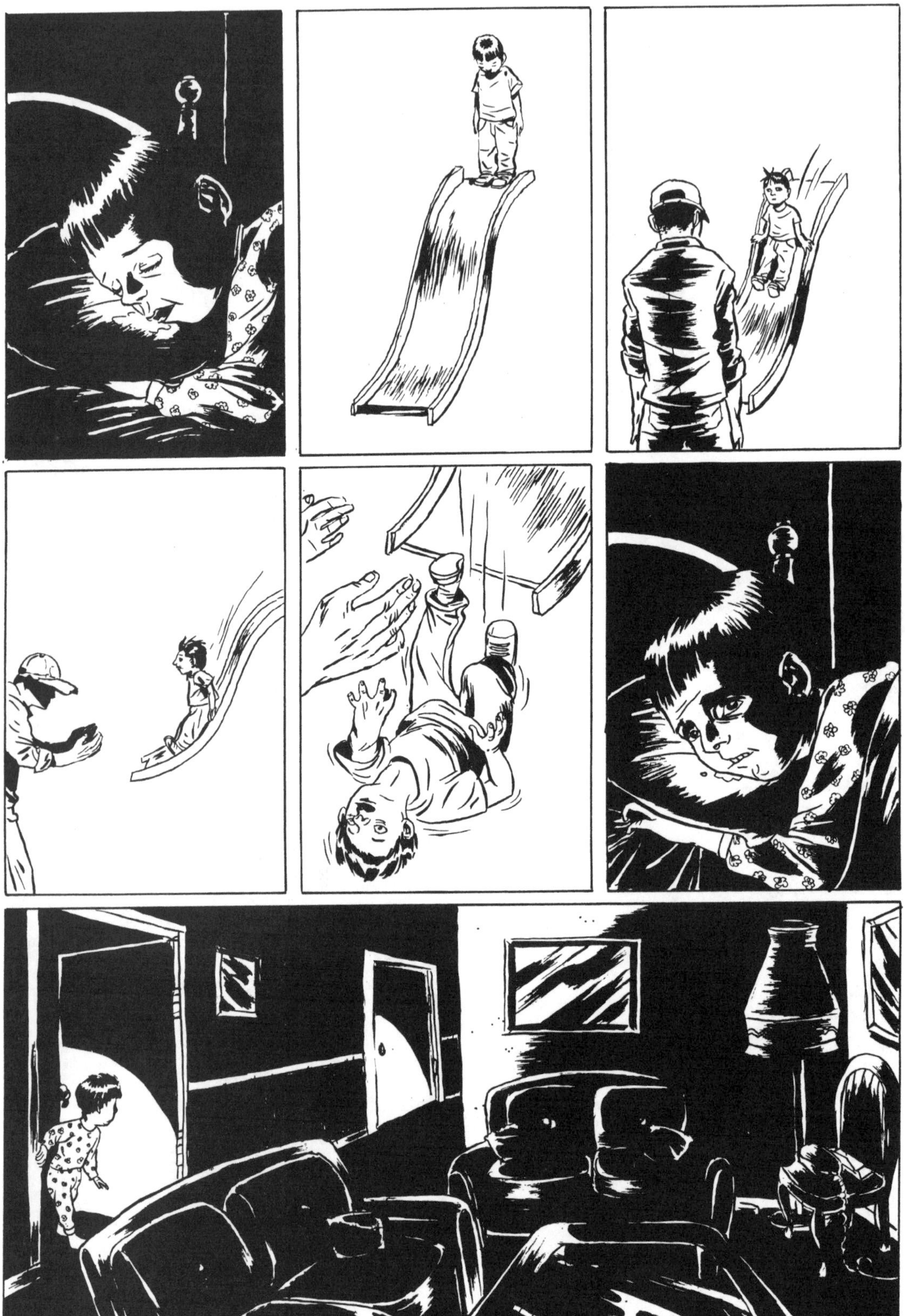

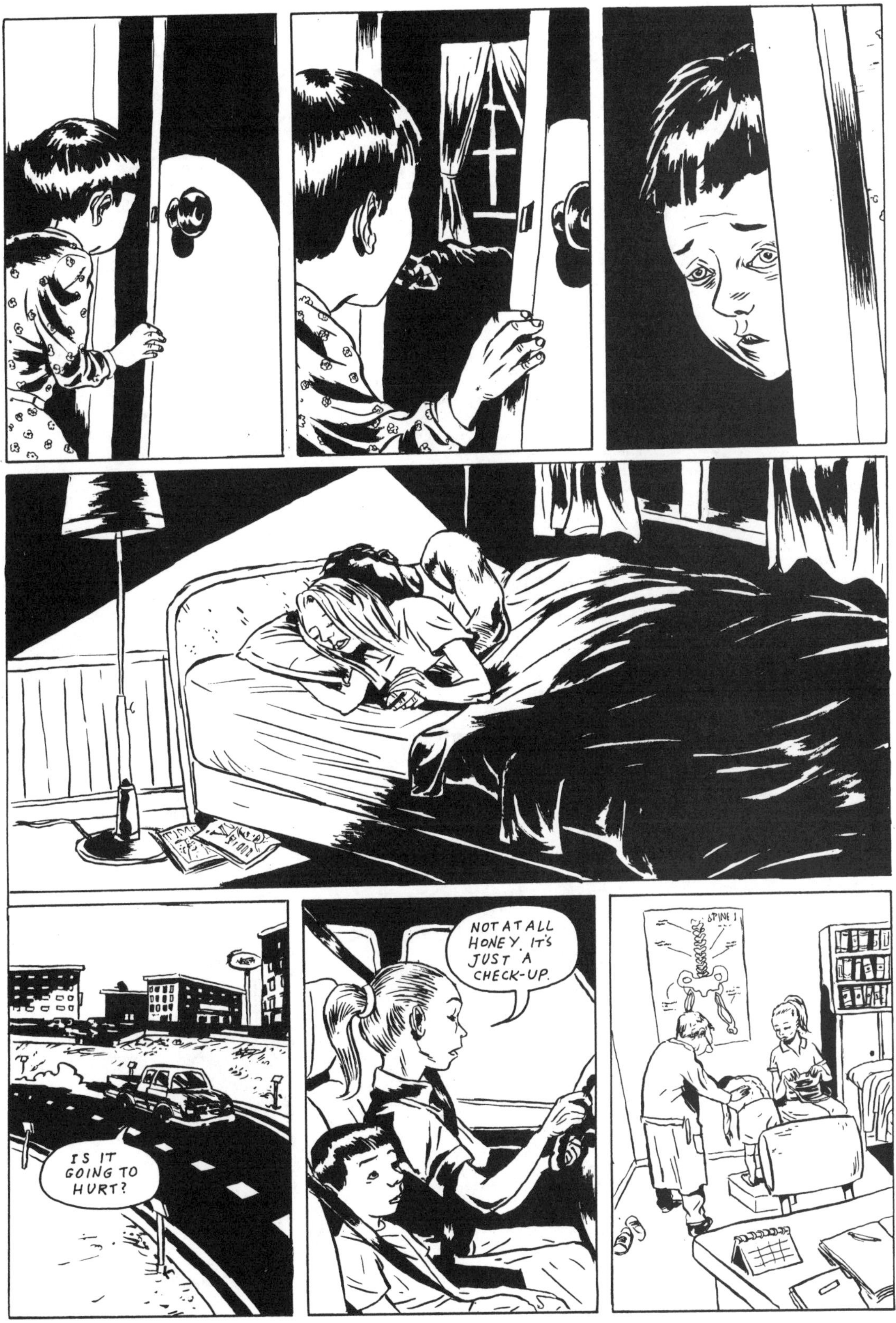
IS IT GOING TO HURT?
NOT AT ALL HONEY. IT'S JUST A CHECK-UP.
SPINE

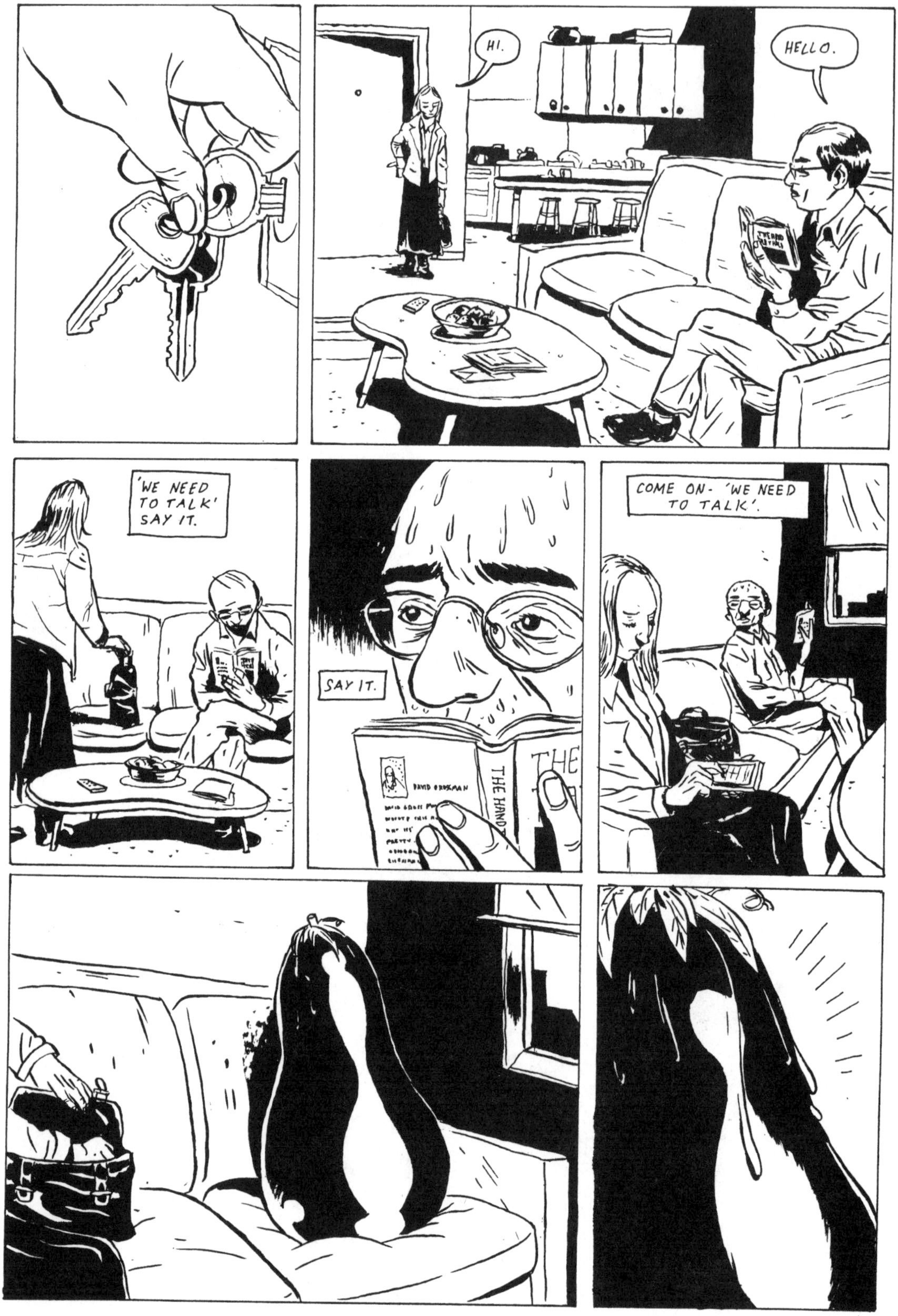
HI.
HELLO.
'WE NEED TO TALK' SAY IT.
SAY IT.
COME ON- 'WE NEED TO TALK'.

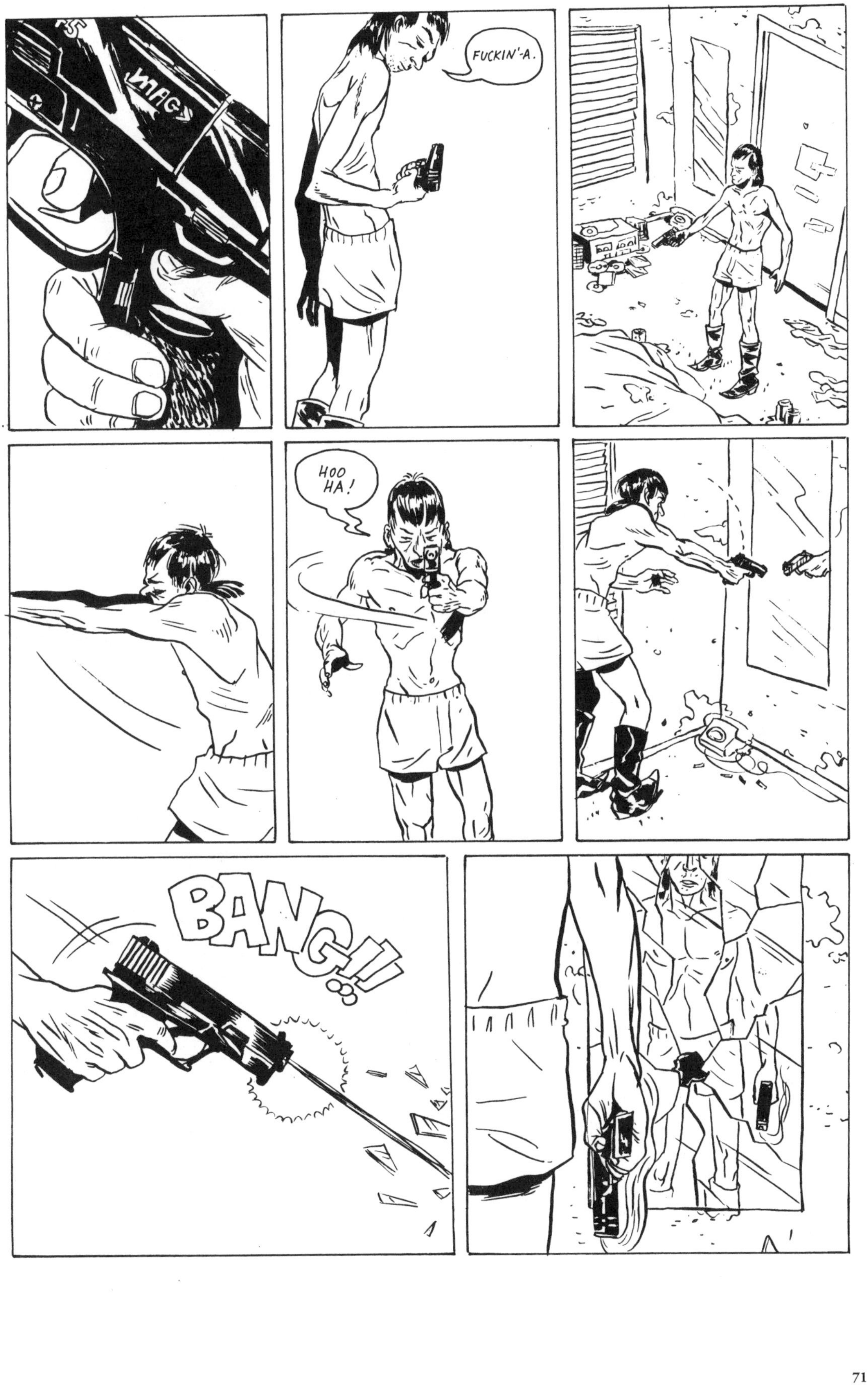
MAG
FUCKIN'-A.
HOO HA!
BANG!!

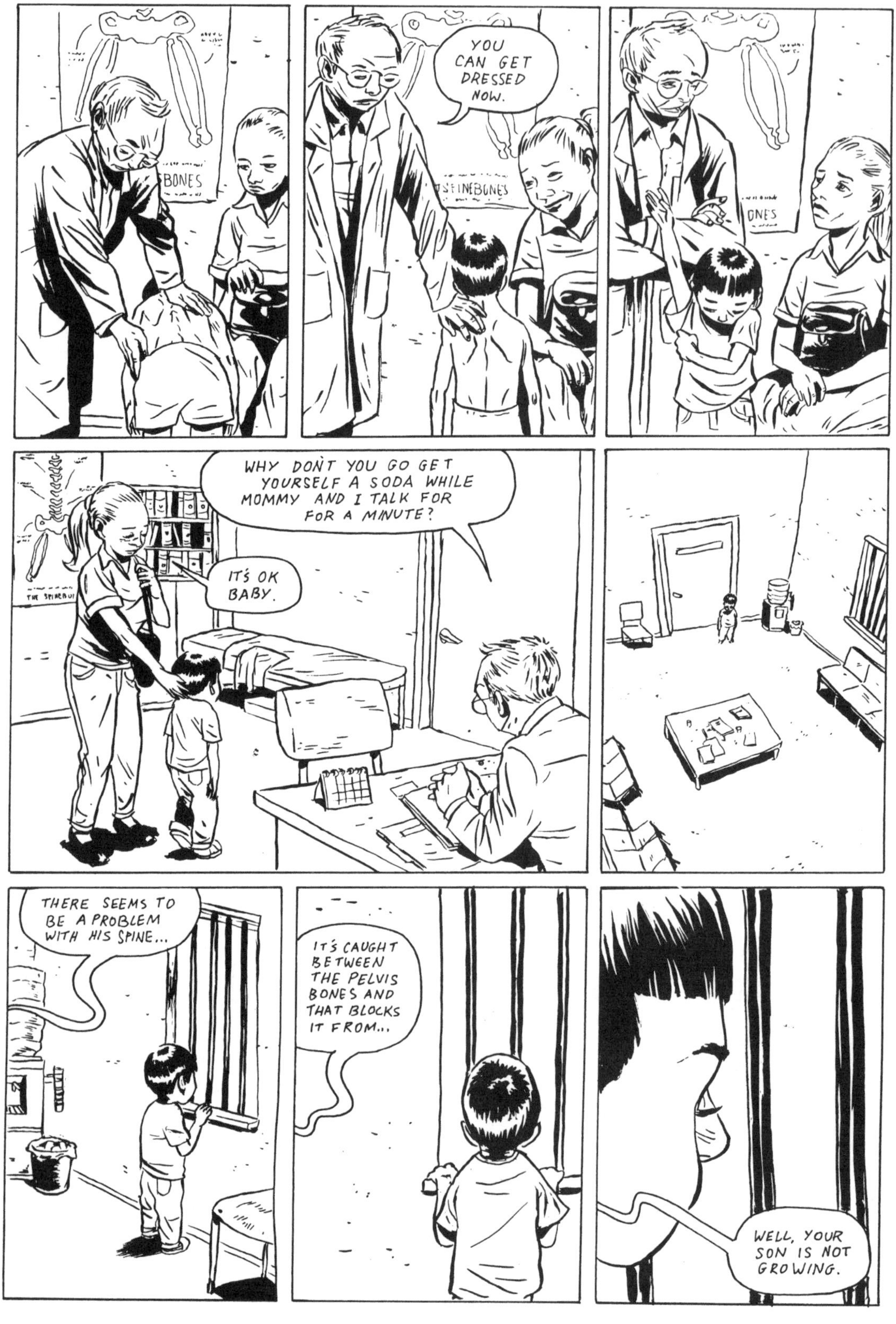
BONES
YOU CAN GET DRESSED NOW.
SPINEBONES
ONES
THE SPINEBO
WHY DON'T YOU GO GET YOURSELF A SODA WHILE MOMMY AND I TALK FOR FOR A MINUTE?
IT'S OK BABY.
THERE SEEMS TO BE A PROBLEM WITH HIS SPINE...
IT'S CAUGHT BETWEEN THE PELVIS BONES AND THAT BLOCKS IT FROM...
WELL, YOUR SON IS NOT GROWING.

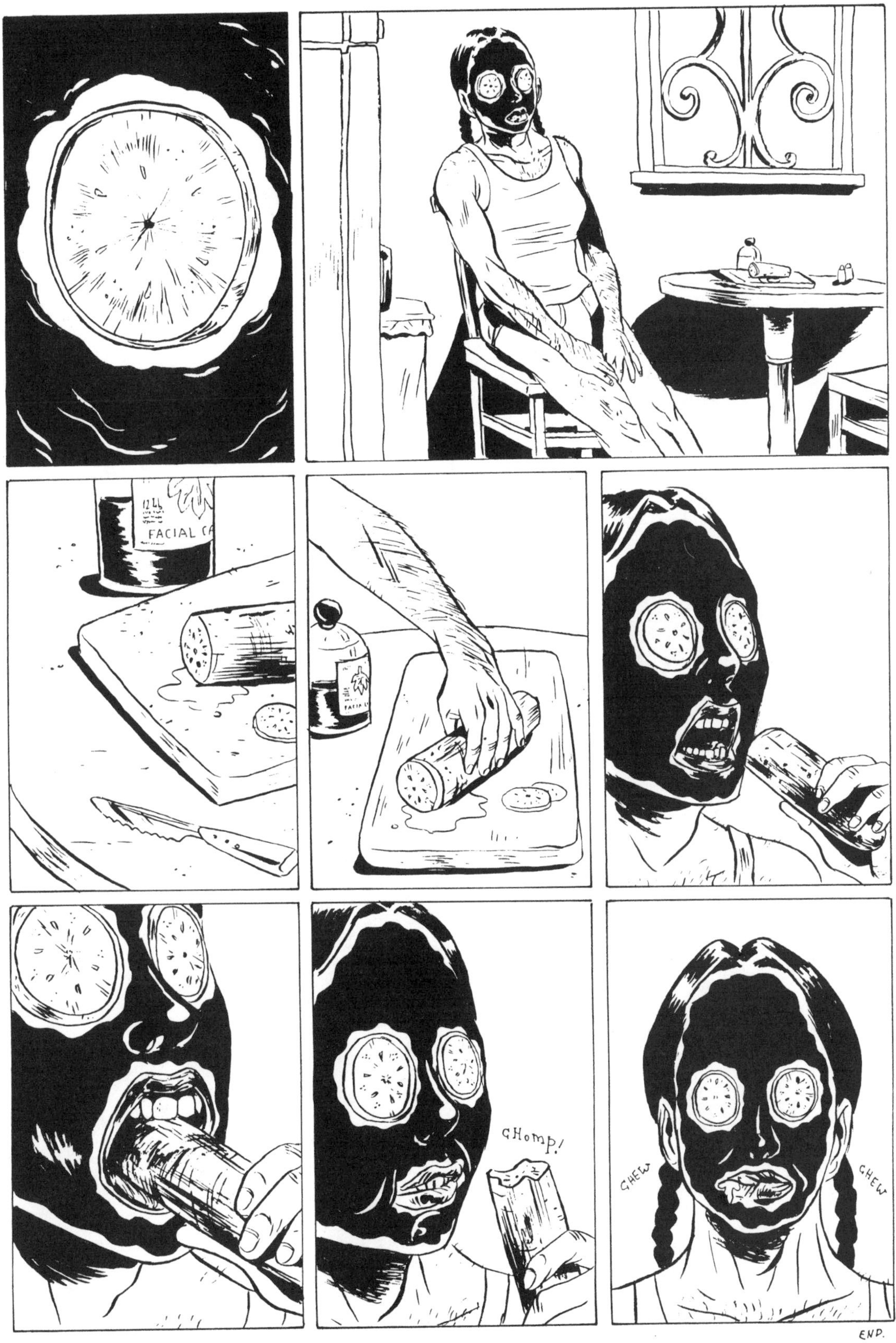
FACIAL CA
CHomp!
CHEW
CHEW

END.

Zina & Me

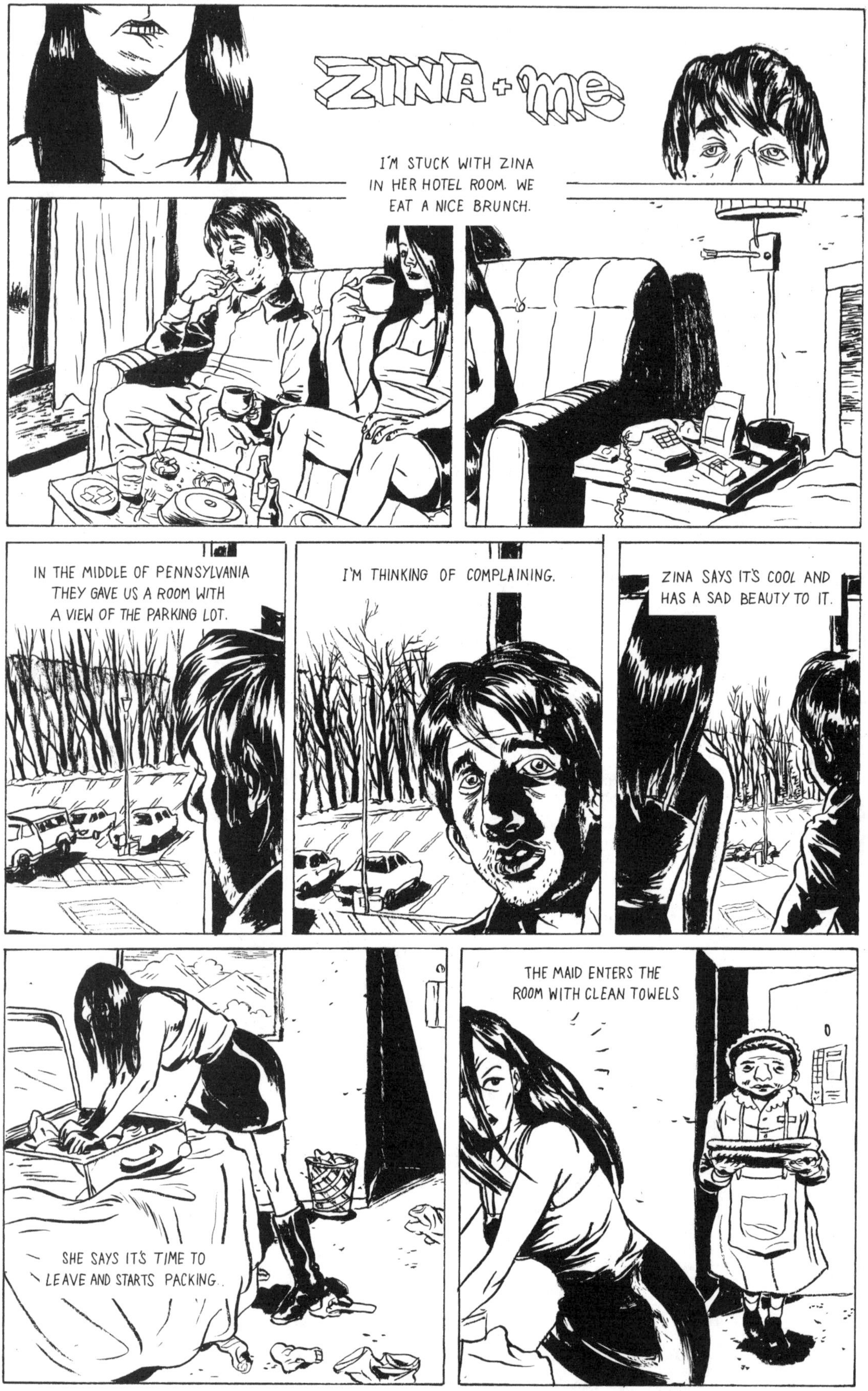
ZINA + me
I'M STUCK WITH ZINA IN HER HOTEL ROOM. WE EAT A NICE BRUNCH.
IN THE MIDDLE OF PENNSYLVANIA THEY GAVE US A ROOM WITH A VIEW OF THE PARKING LOT.
I'M THINKING OF COMPLAINING.
ZINA SAYS IT'S COOL AND HAS A SAD BEAUTY TO IT.
SHE SAYS IT'S TIME TO LEAVE AND STARTS PACKING.
THE MAID ENTERS THE ROOM WITH CLEAN TOWELS

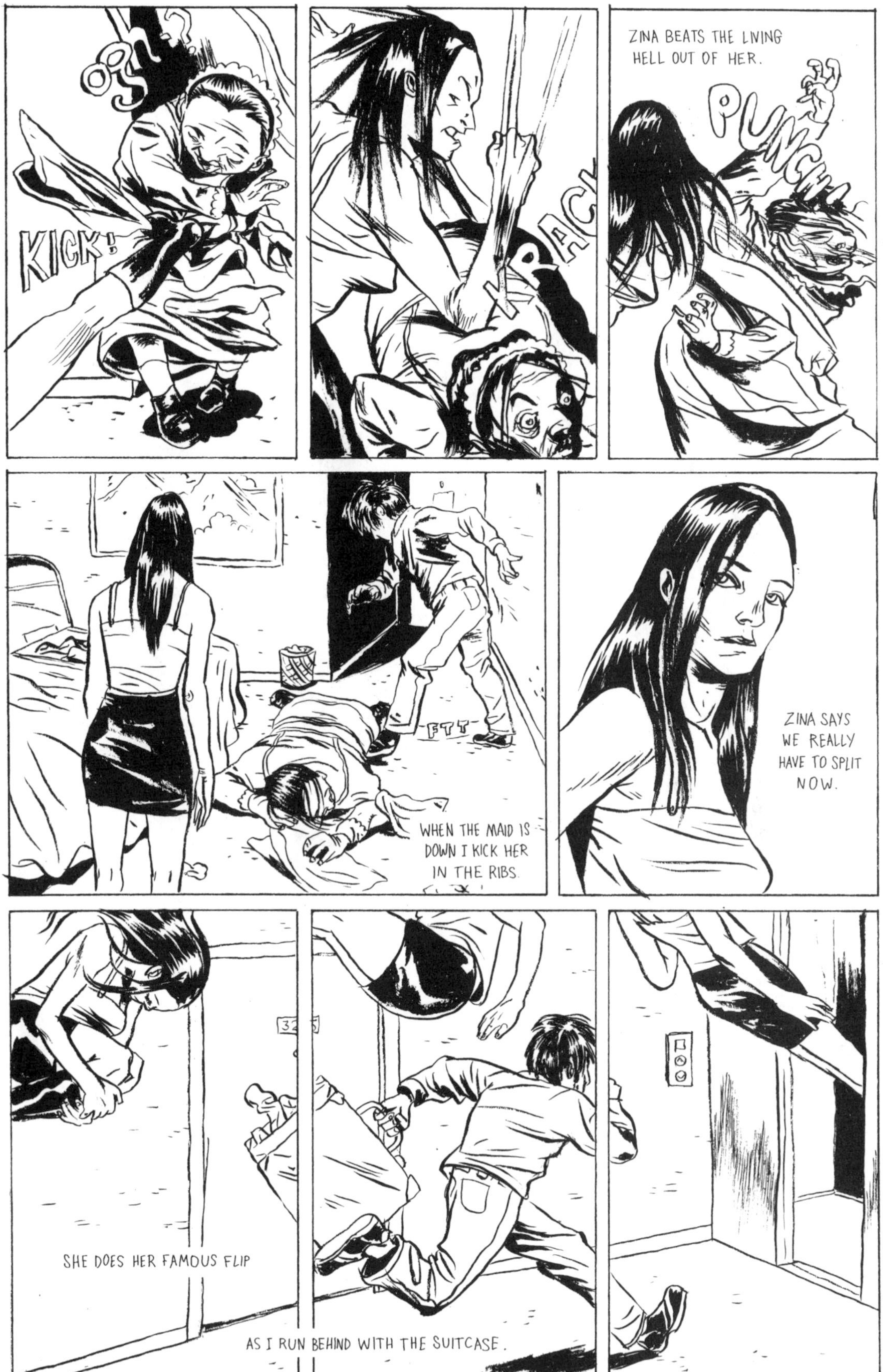

OOGH?
KICK!
KRACK
ZINA BEATS THE LIVING HELL OUT OF HER.
PUNCH
FTT
WHEN THE MAID IS DOWN I KICK HER IN THE RIBS.
ZINA SAYS WE REALLY HAVE TO SPLIT NOW.
SHE DOES HER FAMOUS FLIP
AS I RUN BEHIND WITH THE SUITCASE.

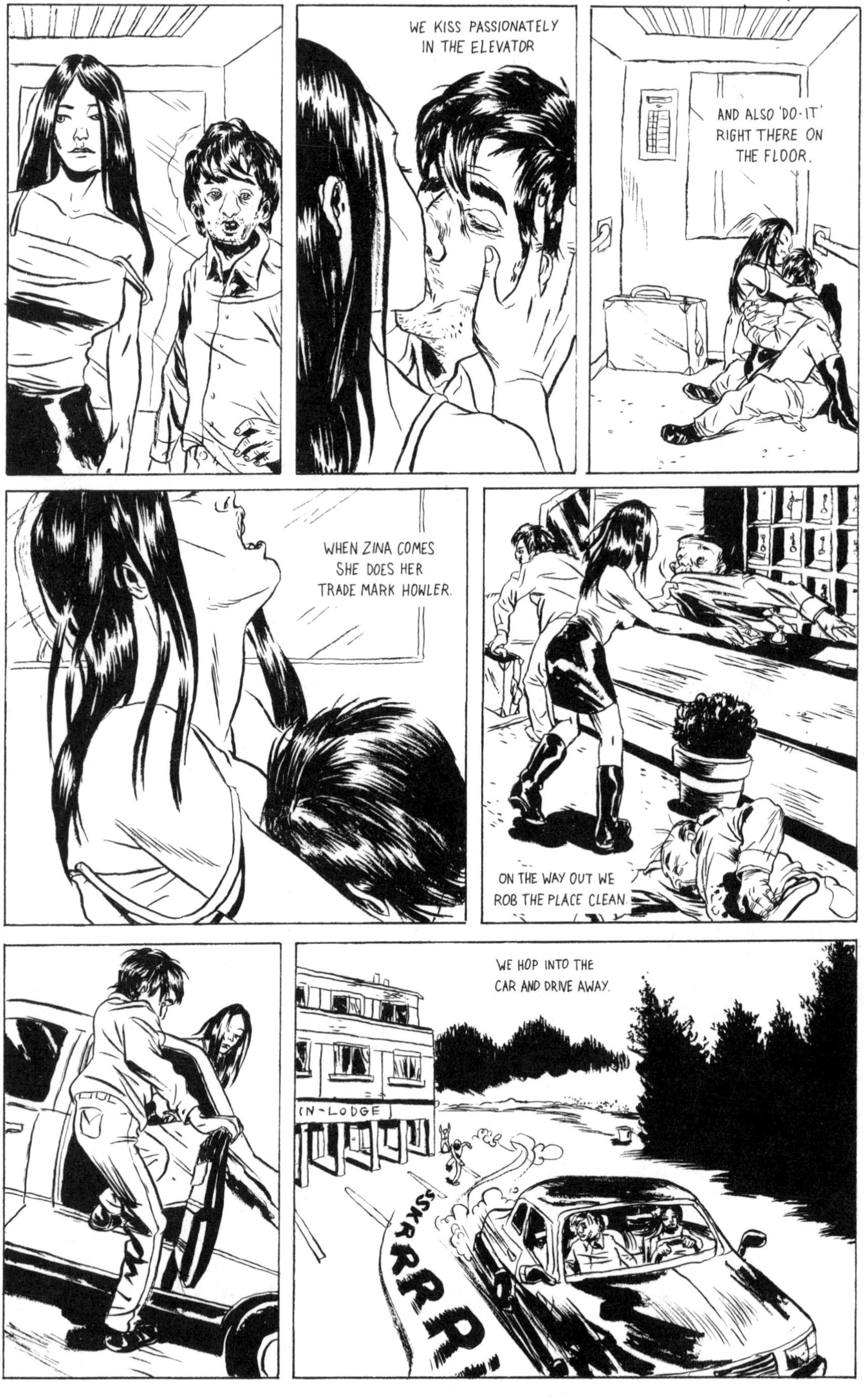
WE KISS PASSIONATELY IN THE ELEVATOR
AND ALSO 'DO-IT' RIGHT THERE ON THE FLOOR.
WHEN ZINA COMES SHE DOES HER TRADE MARK HOWLER.
ON THE WAY OUT WE ROB THE PLACE CLEAN.
WE HOP INTO THE CAR AND DRIVE AWAY.
SSKRRRR

WE DRIVE FOR A WHILE. ZINA ASKS FOR A CIGARETTE.

BUT I'M OUT.

SO SHE SAYS - WHAT GOOD ARE YOU ANYWAY?

AND I SAY CAUSE I'LL ALWAYS BE THERE FOR YOU-

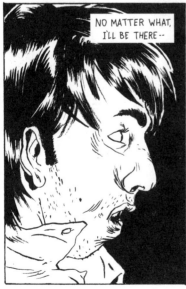

NO MATTER WHAT, I'LL BE THERE --

AND SHE SAYS-REALLY? YOU AND WHAT ARMY?

END.

Telekinetic

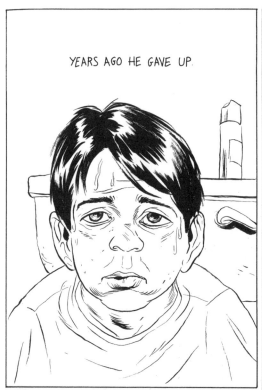

YEARS AGO HE GAVE UP.

SPENDING SO MUCH TIME IN THAT LITTLE ROOM, HOPING THE KNOT IN HIS STOMACH WOULD COME UNTIED, HE HAD DEVELOPED A BELIEF SYSTEM WHICH SUGGESTED THAT ALL PAIN COULD BE SUPPRESSED IF HE HAD THE ABILITY TO MOVE OBJECTS USING ONLY 'BRAIN WAVES'.

TELEKINESIS DID EXIST.
ROBERTO SHMILOVE (1848-1932) HAD 'LIFTED' HIS DAUGHTER MARIA FROM THEIR BURNING HOUSE, AND SO SAVED HER LIFE.

HIS WIFE AND YOUNGER DAUGHTER WITNESSED THIS ASTONISHING EVENT.

ANYWAY, THAT DAY, WHEN HE GAVE TELEKINESIS ITS LAST CHANCE TO MANIFEST ITSELF (IT DIDN'T) WAS THE DAY HE GAVE UP.

ALSO, HE DECIDED THERE WAS NO GOD.

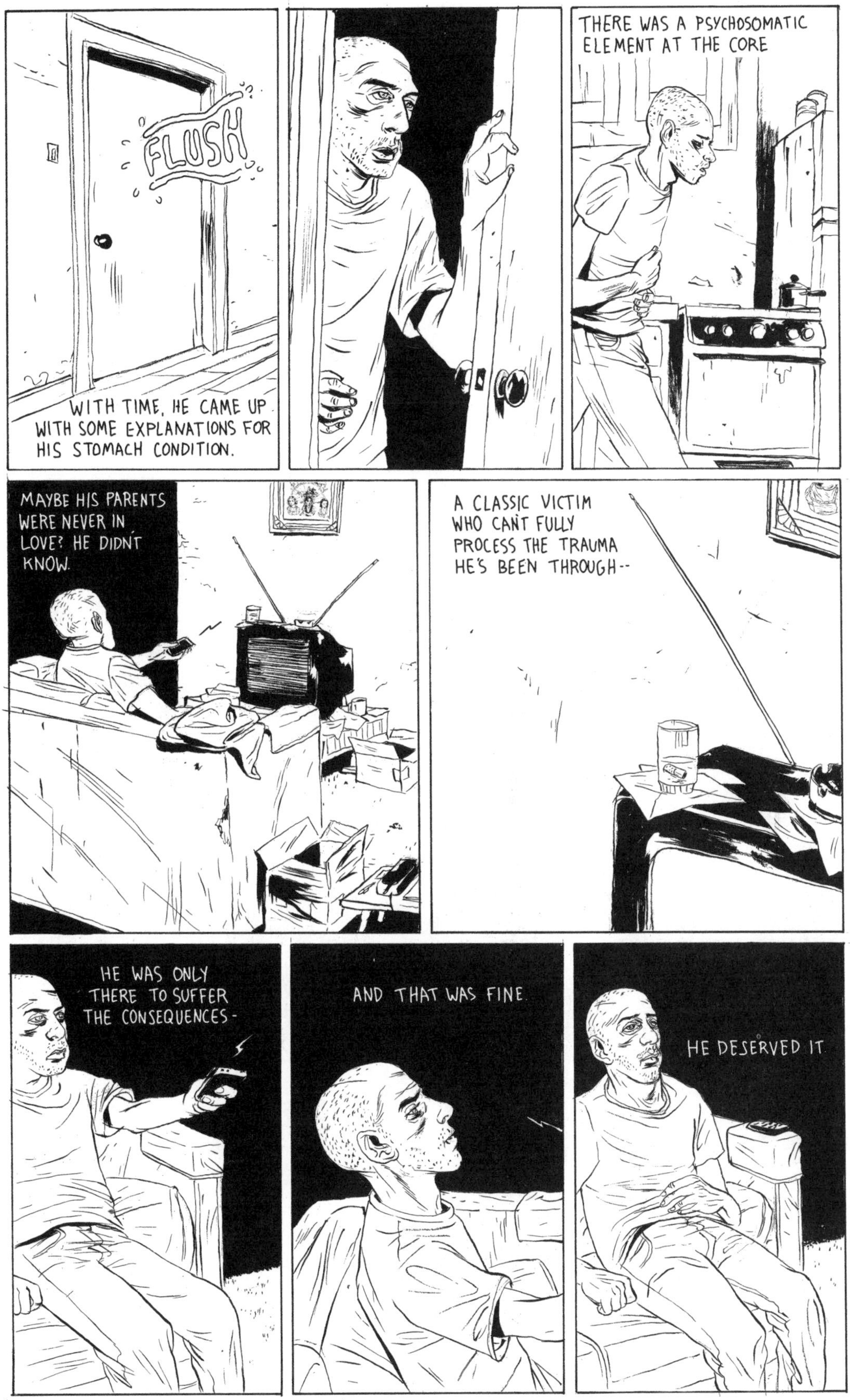
FLUSH
WITH TIME, HE CAME UP WITH SOME EXPLANATIONS FOR HIS STOMACH CONDITION.
THERE WAS A PSYCHOSOMATIC ELEMENT AT THE CORE
MAYBE HIS PARENTS WERE NEVER IN LOVE? HE DIDN'T KNOW.
A CLASSIC VICTIM WHO CAN'T FULLY PROCESS THE TRAUMA HE'S BEEN THROUGH--
HE WAS ONLY THERE TO SUFFER THE CONSEQUENCES-
AND THAT WAS FINE.
HE DESERVED IT.

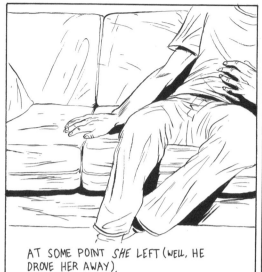

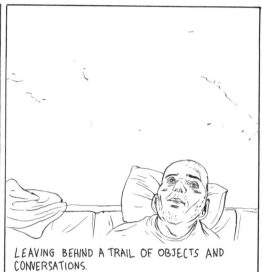

AT SOME POINT *SHE* LEFT (WELL, HE DROVE HER AWAY),

LEAVING BEHIND A TRAIL OF OBJECTS AND CONVERSATIONS.

WHAT DO YOU MEAN, 'WHAT DO YOU WANT'?

HE KEPT FOLLOWING THIS TRAIL IN CIRCLES, RECITING OLD CONVERSATIONS OVER AND OVER.

WITHOUT YOU NOTHING MAKES SENSE.

SOMETIMES TAKING THE LIBERTY OF EDITING-

HE DECONSTRUCTED SENTEN-CES, ADDING WORDS THAT SHOULD HAVE BEEN SAID.

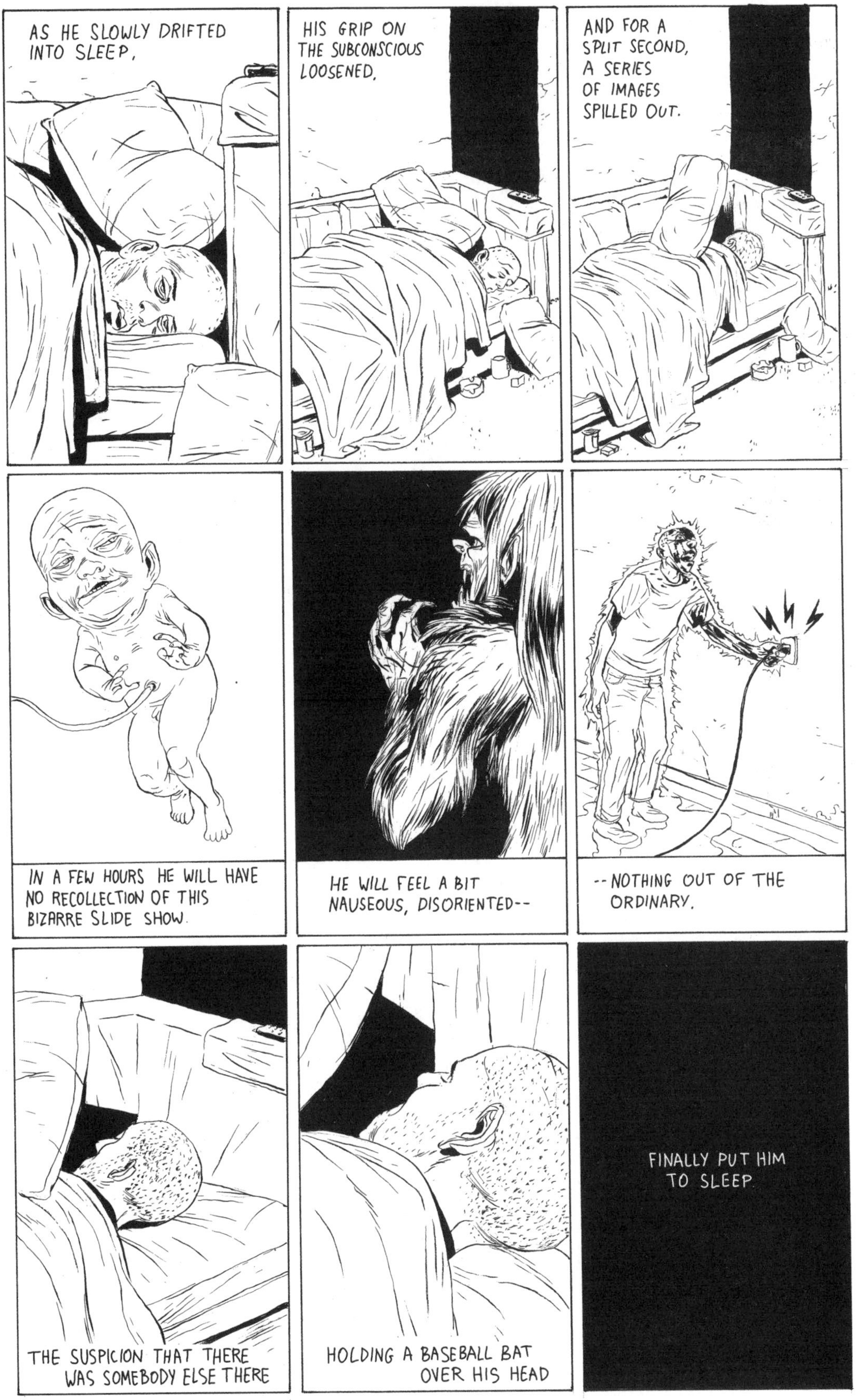
AS HE SLOWLY DRIFTED INTO SLEEP,
HIS GRIP ON THE SUBCONSCIOUS LOOSENED,
AND FOR A SPLIT SECOND, A SERIES OF IMAGES SPILLED OUT.
IN A FEW HOURS HE WILL HAVE NO RECOLLECTION OF THIS BIZARRE SLIDE SHOW.
HE WILL FEEL A BIT NAUSEOUS, DISORIENTED--
--NOTHING OUT OF THE ORDINARY.
THE SUSPICION THAT THERE WAS SOMEBODY ELSE THERE
HOLDING A BASEBALL BAT OVER HIS HEAD
FINALLY PUT HIM TO SLEEP.

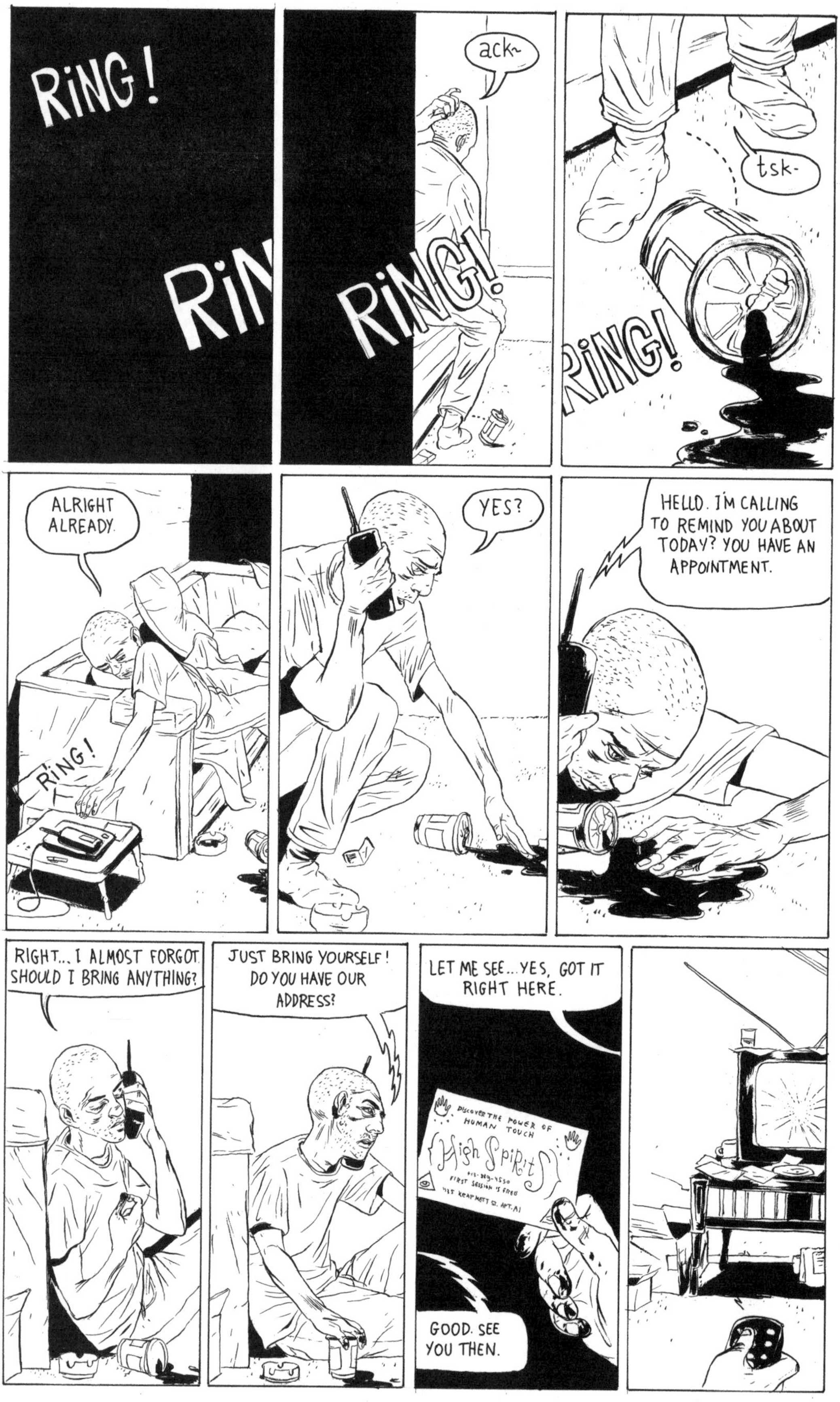

RiNG!
RiN
RiNG!
ack~
tsk-
RiNG!
ALRIGHT ALREADY.
RiNG!
YES?
HELLO. I'M CALLING TO REMIND YOU ABOUT TODAY? YOU HAVE AN APPOINTMENT.
RIGHT... I ALMOST FORGOT. SHOULD I BRING ANYTHING?
JUST BRING YOURSELF! DO YOU HAVE OUR ADDRESS?
LET ME SEE... YES, GOT IT RIGHT HERE.
DISCOVER THE POWER OF HUMAN TOUCH
High Spirits
FIRST SESSION IS FREE
GOOD. SEE YOU THEN.

A PICTURE ON THE WALL WAS TILTED. HE HADN'T NOTICED IT BEFORE. THE PLACE WAS ALWAYS A MESS,

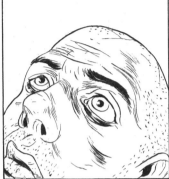

STILL, HE WOULD HAVE NOTICED A MOVING PICTURE.

YESTERDAY, HE RECALLED, THE VOLUME ON THE T.V WENT UP WHILE HE WAS IN THE KITCHEN. OTHER UNEXPLAINED DETAILS WERE EXPOSED:

A PILE OF SAND IN THE BACK ROOM.

A CRACK IN THE KITCHEN WINDOW.

A DROP OF BLOOD IN THE BATHROOM SINK.

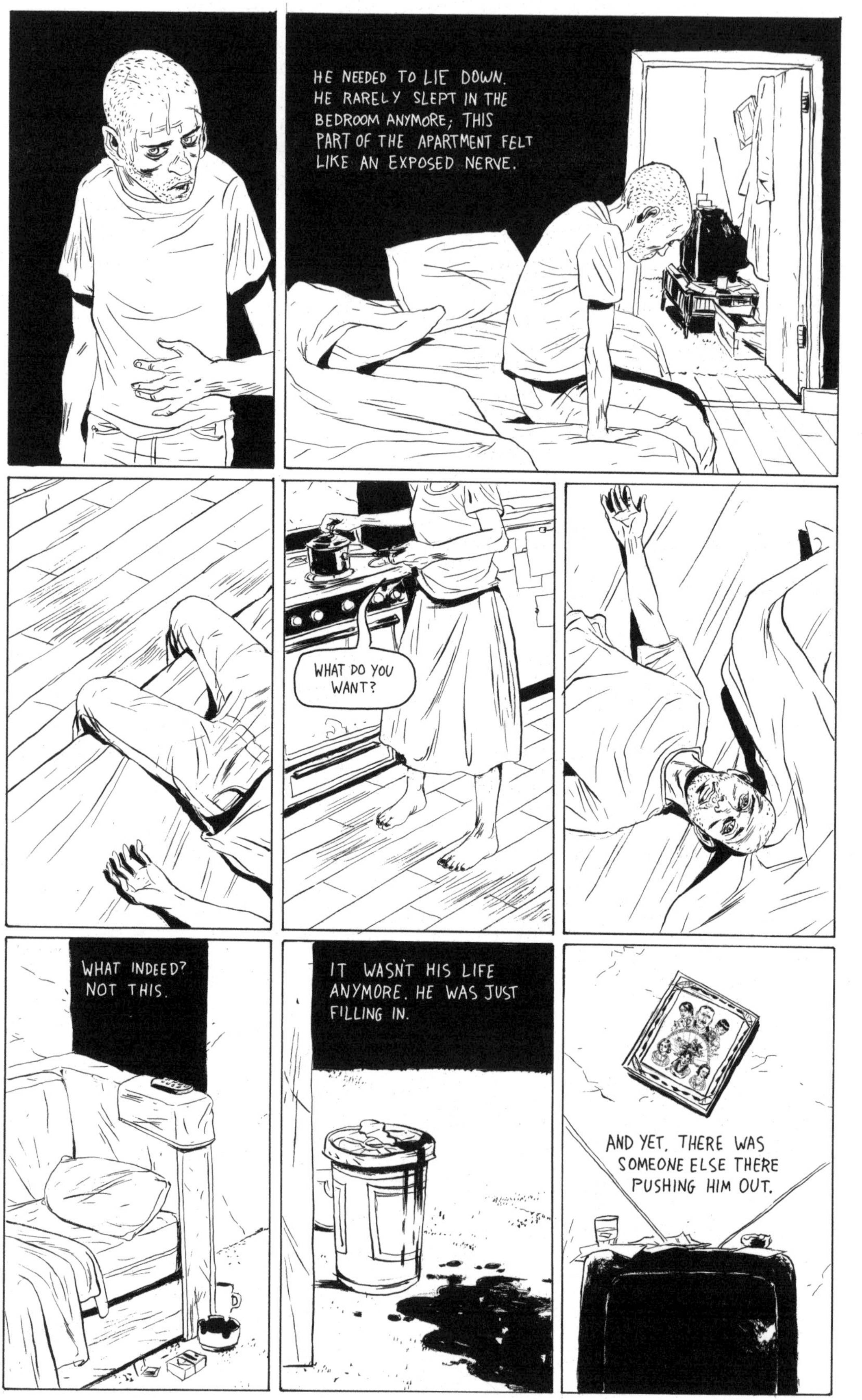
HE NEEDED TO LIE DOWN. HE RARELY SLEPT IN THE BEDROOM ANYMORE; THIS PART OF THE APARTMENT FELT LIKE AN EXPOSED NERVE.
WHAT DO YOU WANT?
WHAT INDEED? NOT THIS.
IT WASN'T HIS LIFE ANYMORE. HE WAS JUST FILLING IN.
AND YET, THERE WAS SOMEONE ELSE THERE PUSHING HIM OUT.

LATE FOR HIS APPOINTMENT, HE DRESSED QUICKLY AND LEFT.

DID HE LEAVE THE COFFEE MAKER ON? OR A CIGARETTE BURNING IN AN ASHTRAY?

IF THE PLACE GOES UP IN FLAMES, NOTHING OF REAL VALUE WOULD BE LOST ANYWAY.

ROBERTO! MARIA IS STILL IN THERE!

AFTER THAT 'LIFTING' STUNT, ROBERTO SHMILOVE BECAME A RENOWNED PSYCHIC.

SHMILOVE

LAUGHING WITH GODS

BUT THE FAMILY WAS RECLUSIVE. NONE OF THE DAUGHTERS GOT MARRIED. NO ONE WAS ALLOWED TO VISIT.

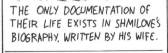

THE ONLY DOCUMENTATION OF THEIR LIFE EXISTS IN SHMILOVE'S BIOGRAPHY, WRITTEN BY HIS WIFE.

IT MENTIONS THAT HIS ABILITY TO LIFT MARIA FROM THE BURNING HOUSE WAS DRIVEN BY HIS GREAT LOVE FOR HER.

BUT WHAT IF HE HADN'T BEEN ABLE TO SAVE HER?

89

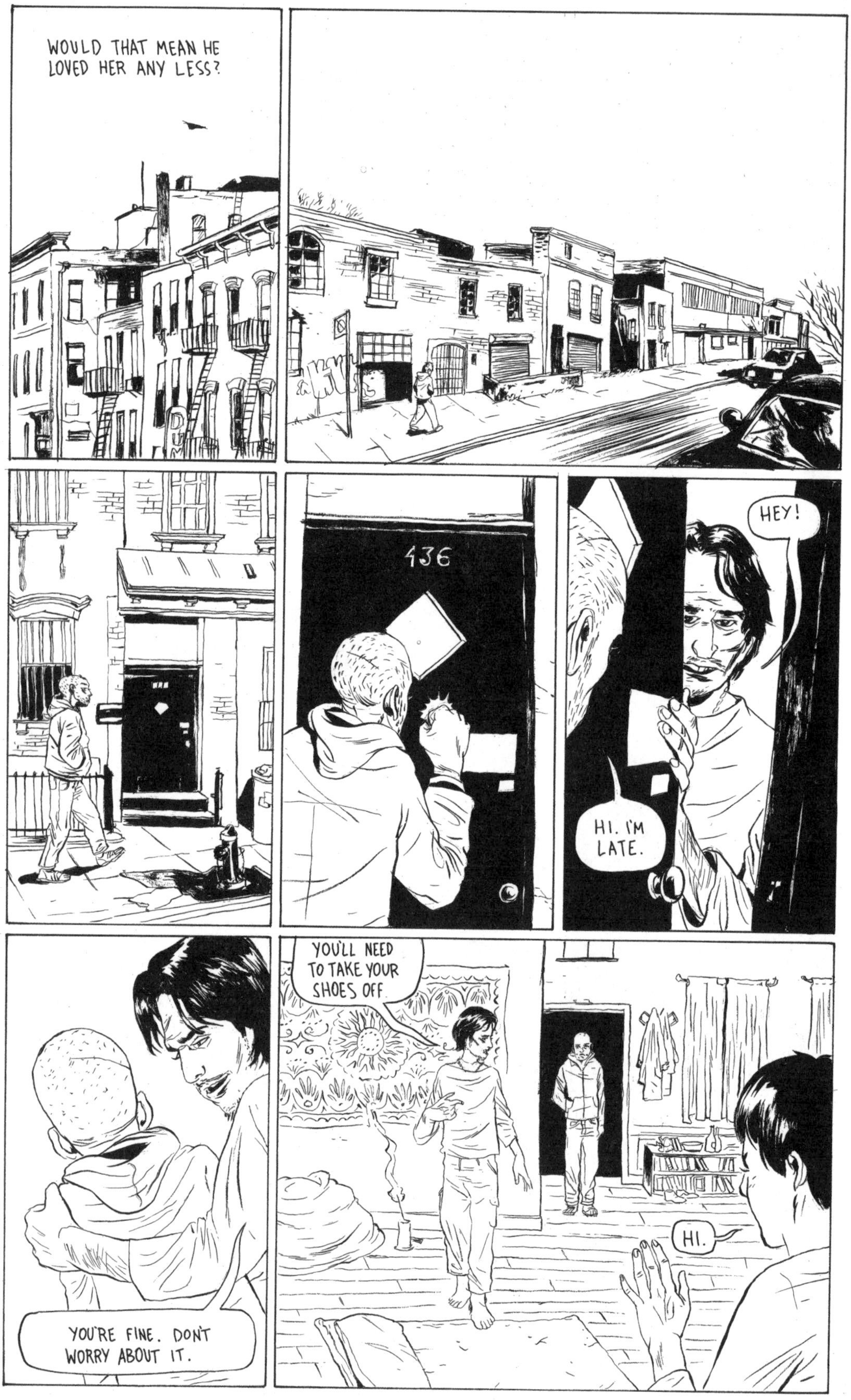
WOULD THAT MEAN HE LOVED HER ANY LESS?
436
HEY!
HI. I'M LATE.
YOU'RE FINE. DON'T WORRY ABOUT IT.
YOU'LL NEED TO TAKE YOUR SHOES OFF.
HI.

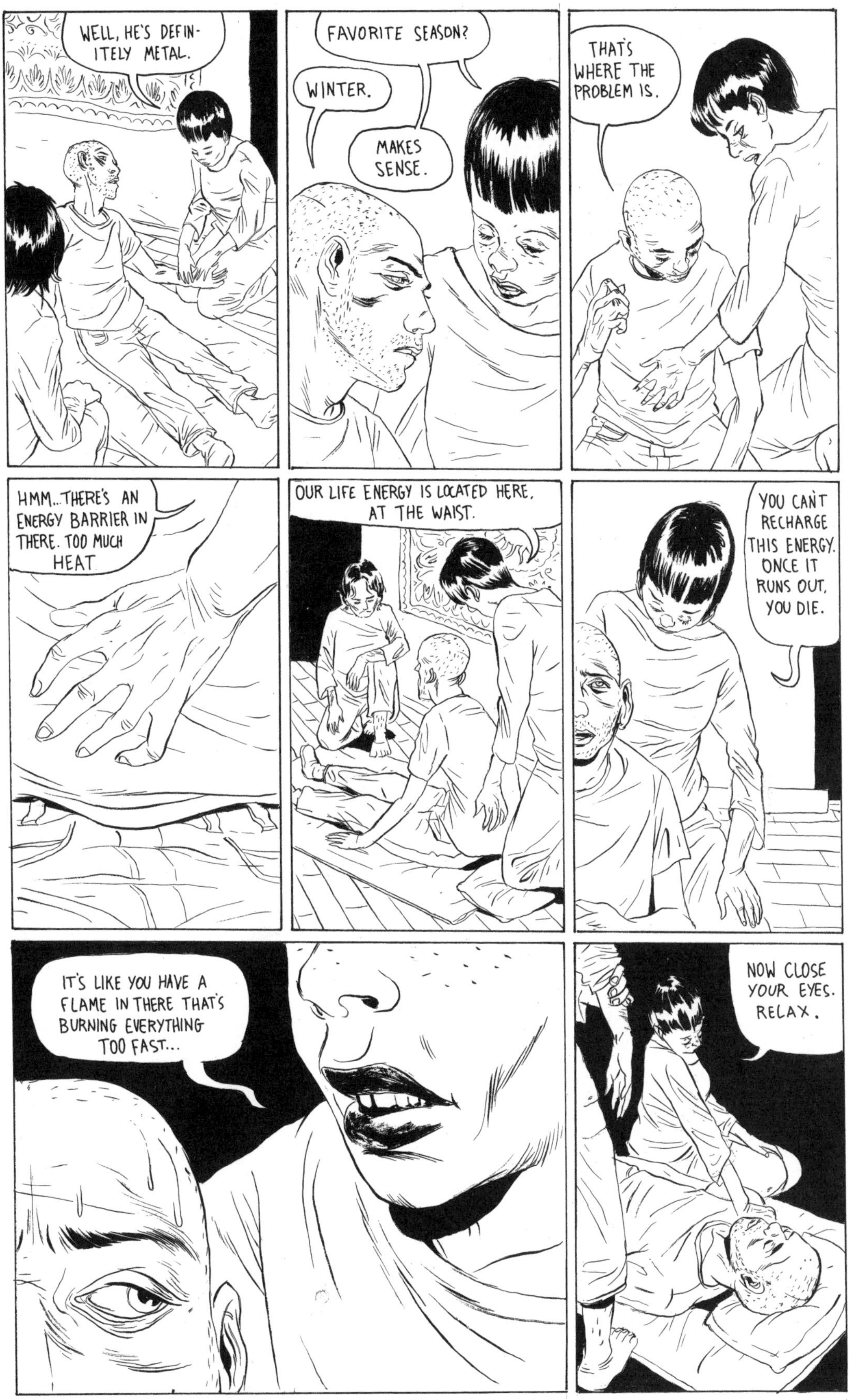
WELL, HE'S DEFIN-ITELY METAL.
FAVORITE SEASON?
WINTER.
MAKES SENSE.
THAT'S WHERE THE PROBLEM IS.
HMM... THERE'S AN ENERGY BARRIER IN THERE. TOO MUCH HEAT
OUR LIFE ENERGY IS LOCATED HERE, AT THE WAIST.
YOU CAN'T RECHARGE THIS ENERGY. ONCE IT RUNS OUT, YOU DIE.
IT'S LIKE YOU HAVE A FLAME IN THERE THAT'S BURNING EVERYTHING TOO FAST...
NOW CLOSE YOUR EYES. RELAX.

THINK ABOUT NOTHING.

SHE'S STILL IN THERE...

AT SOME POINT MARIA KILLS HERSELF. SHMILOVE IS ALREADY GONE (HE DIED OF NATURAL CAUSES). THE YOUNGER SISTER NATASHA FINDS A FAREWELL LETTER ON MARIA'S DESK. IT WAS QUOTED IN THE BIOGRAPHY--

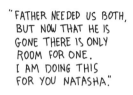

"FATHER NEEDED US BOTH, BUT NOW THAT HE IS GONE THERE IS ONLY ROOM FOR ONE. I AM DOING THIS FOR YOU NATASHA."

POOR NATASHA.

DOES IT MAKE YOU FEEL ANY BETTER?

DOWN THERE. HOW DOES IT FEEL?

LIKE A DEAD BABY.

HE COULDN'T WAIT TO GET BACK HOME. MAKE SOME COFFEE. WATCH T.V.

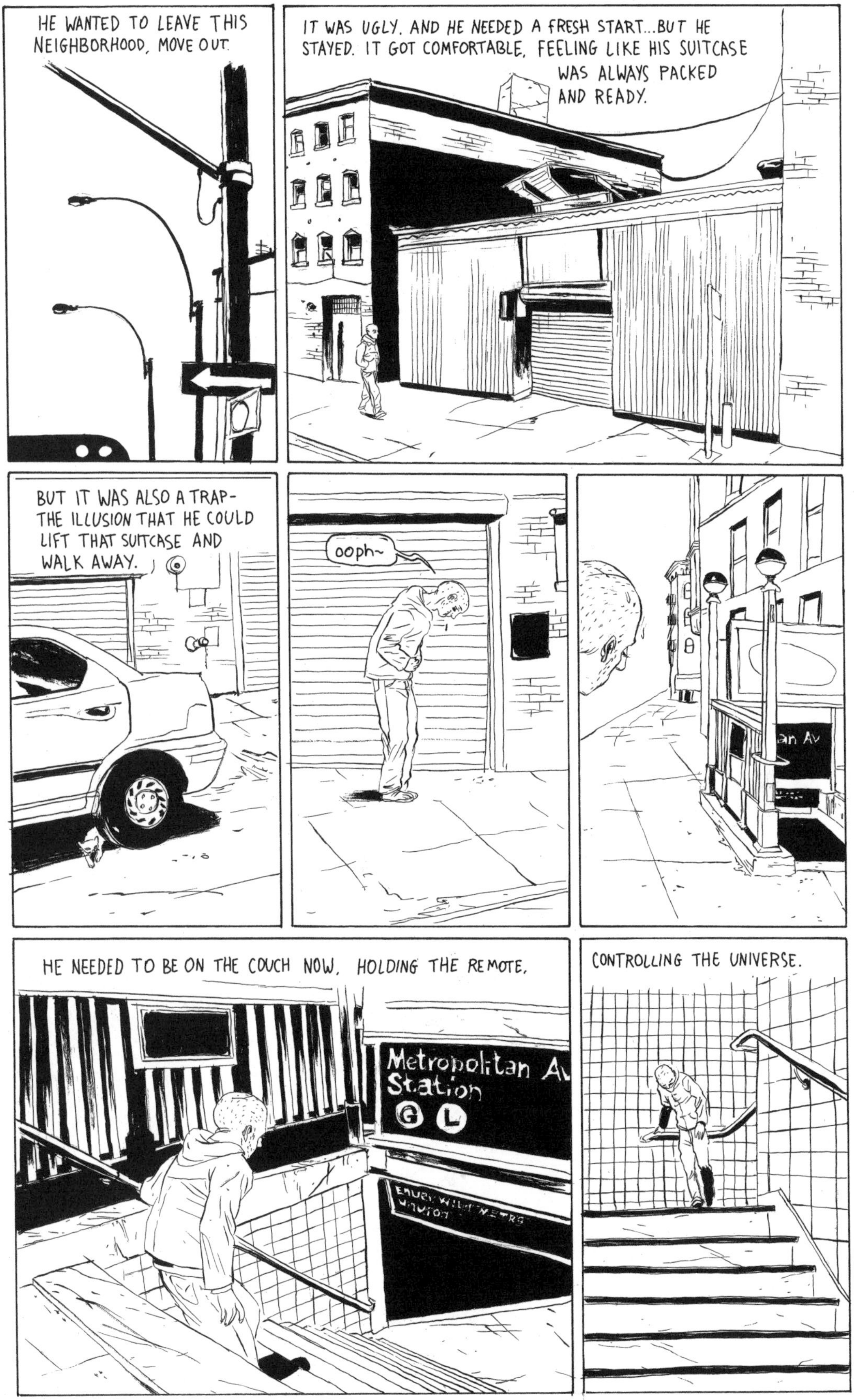

HE WANTED TO LEAVE THIS NEIGHBORHOOD, MOVE OUT.
IT WAS UGLY. AND HE NEEDED A FRESH START...BUT HE STAYED. IT GOT COMFORTABLE, FEELING LIKE HIS SUITCASE WAS ALWAYS PACKED AND READY.
BUT IT WAS ALSO A TRAP- THE ILLUSION THAT HE COULD LIFT THAT SUITCASE AND WALK AWAY.
ooph~
an Av
HE NEEDED TO BE ON THE COUCH NOW, HOLDING THE REMOTE,
Metropolitan Av
Station
G
L
CONTROLLING THE UNIVERSE.

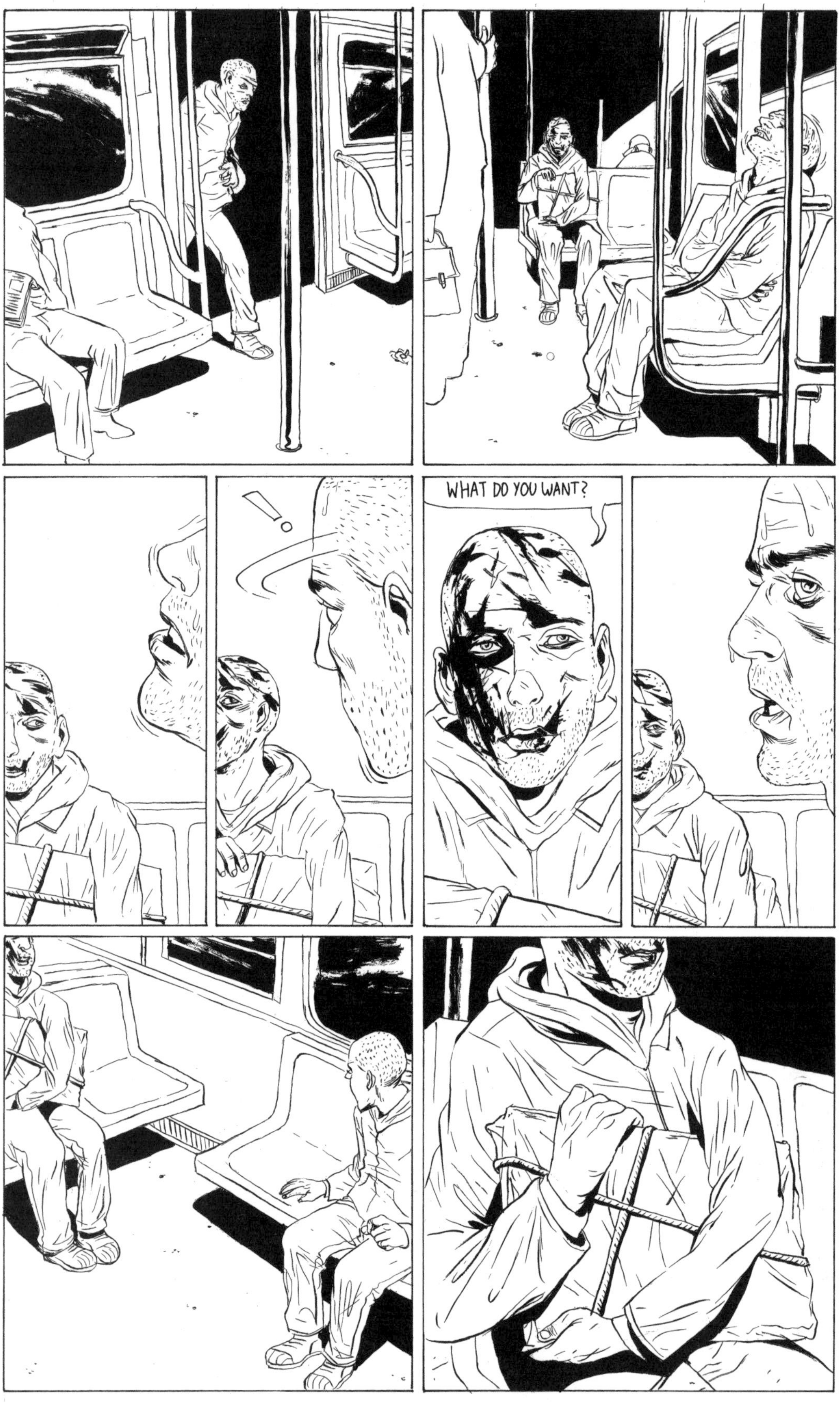
!
WHAT DO YOU WANT?

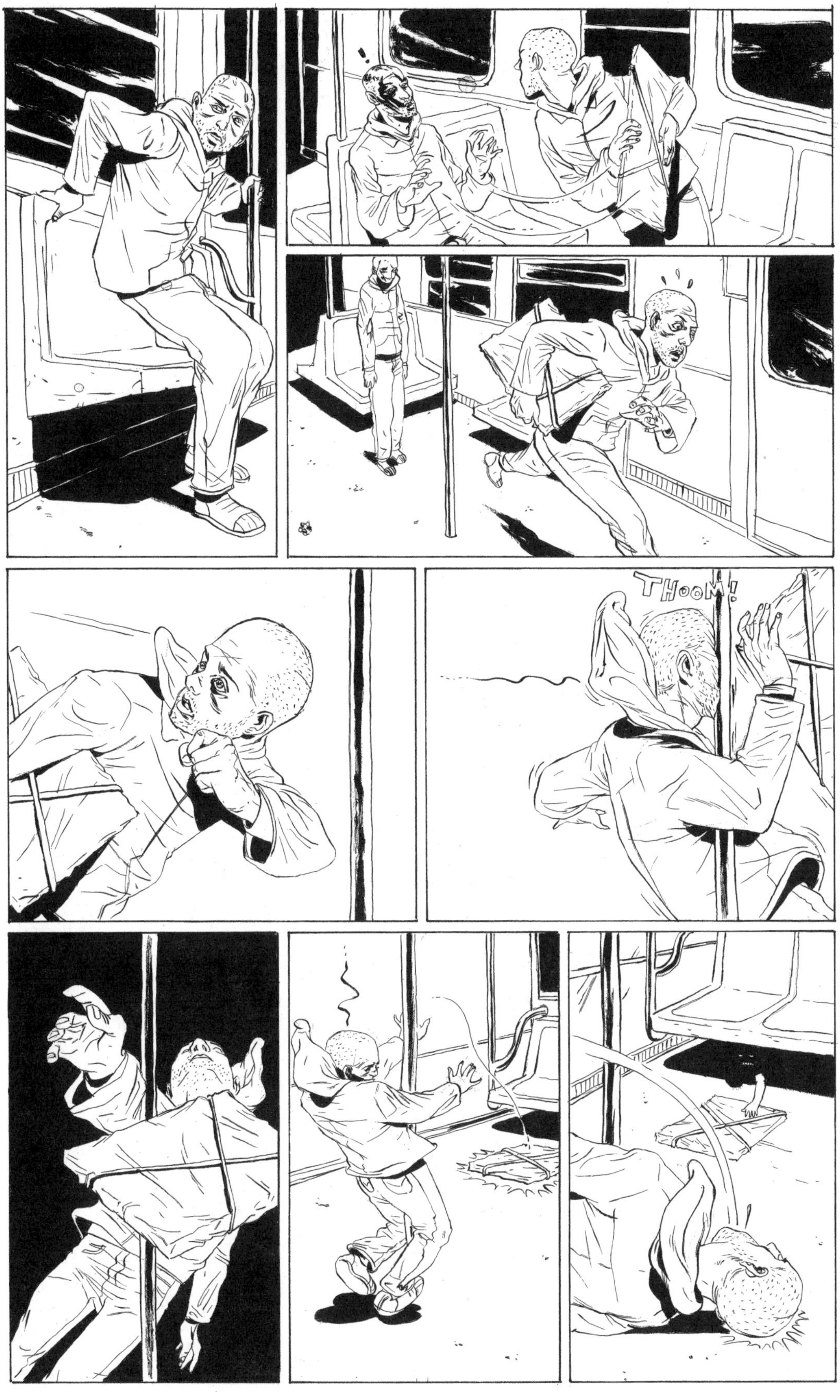
THOOM!

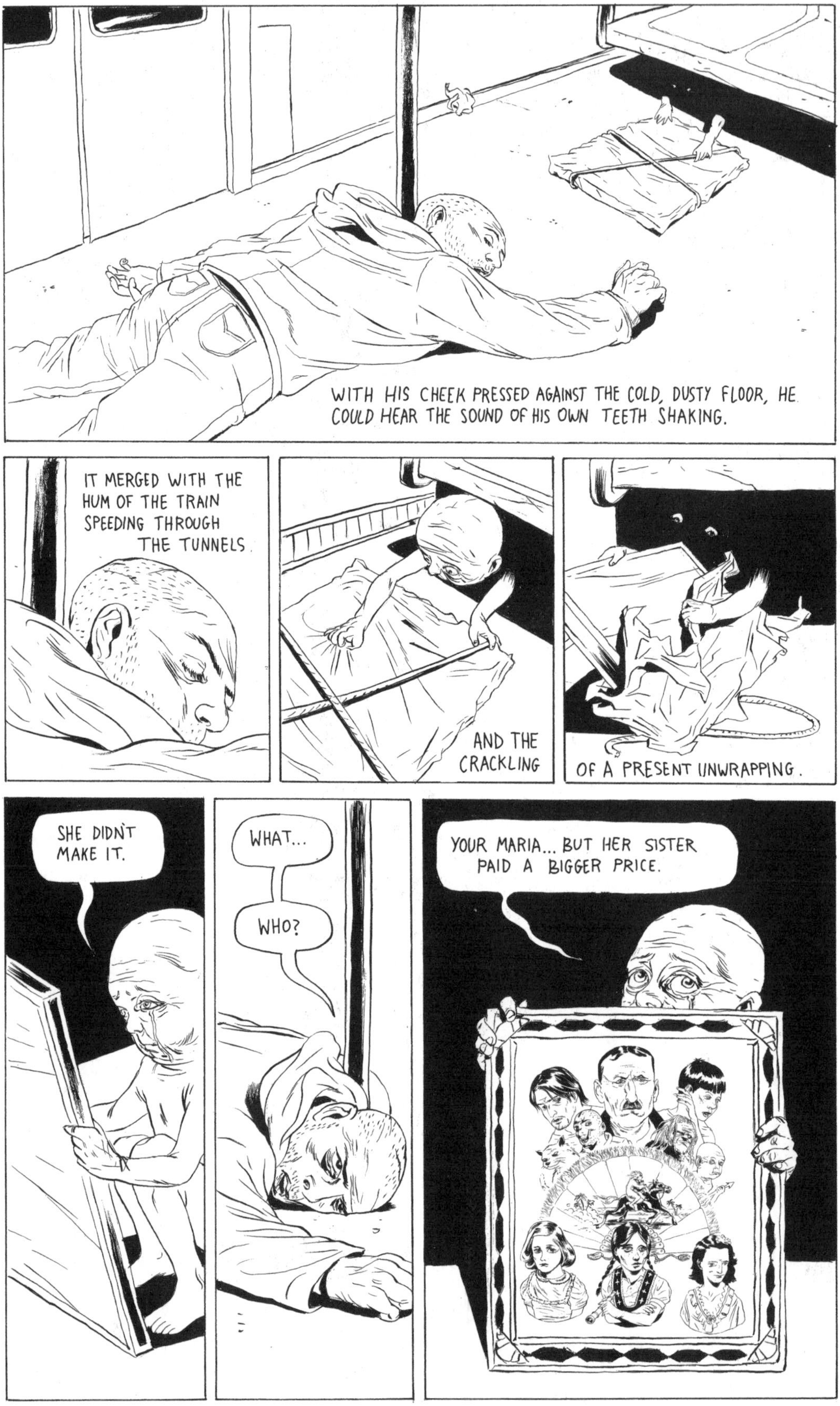
WITH HIS CHEEK PRESSED AGAINST THE COLD, DUSTY FLOOR, HE COULD HEAR THE SOUND OF HIS OWN TEETH SHAKING.
IT MERGED WITH THE HUM OF THE TRAIN SPEEDING THROUGH THE TUNNELS
AND THE CRACKLING
OF A PRESENT UNWRAPPING.
SHE DIDN'T MAKE IT.
WHAT...
WHO?
YOUR MARIA... BUT HER SISTER PAID A BIGGER PRICE.

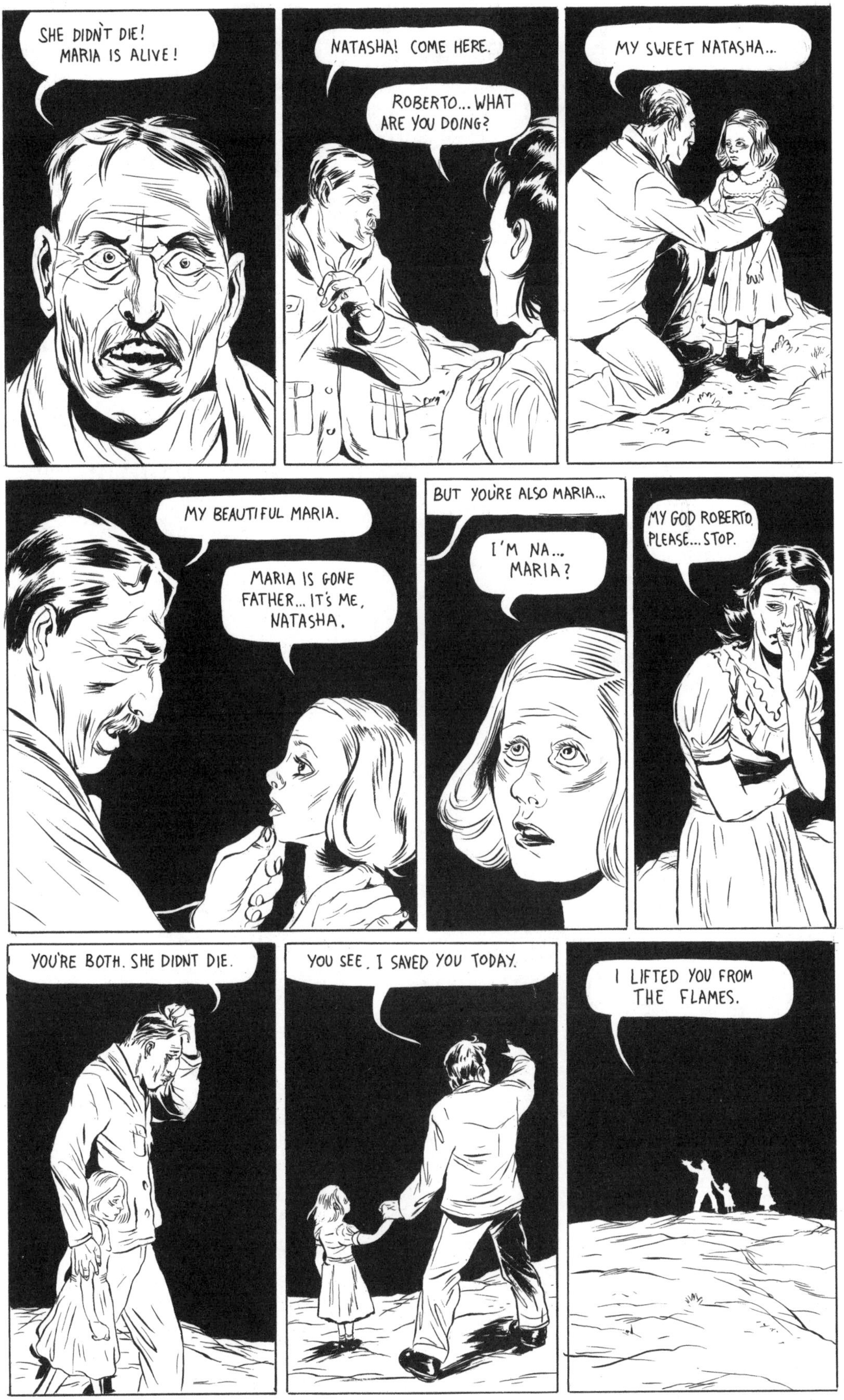
SHE DIDN'T DIE! MARIA IS ALIVE!
NATASHA! COME HERE.
ROBERTO... WHAT ARE YOU DOING?
MY SWEET NATASHA...
MY BEAUTIFUL MARIA.
MARIA IS GONE FATHER... IT'S ME, NATASHA.
BUT YOU'RE ALSO MARIA...
I'M NA... MARIA?
MY GOD ROBERTO. PLEASE... STOP.
YOU'RE BOTH. SHE DIDNT DIE.
YOU SEE. I SAVED YOU TODAY.
I LIFTED YOU FROM THE FLAMES.

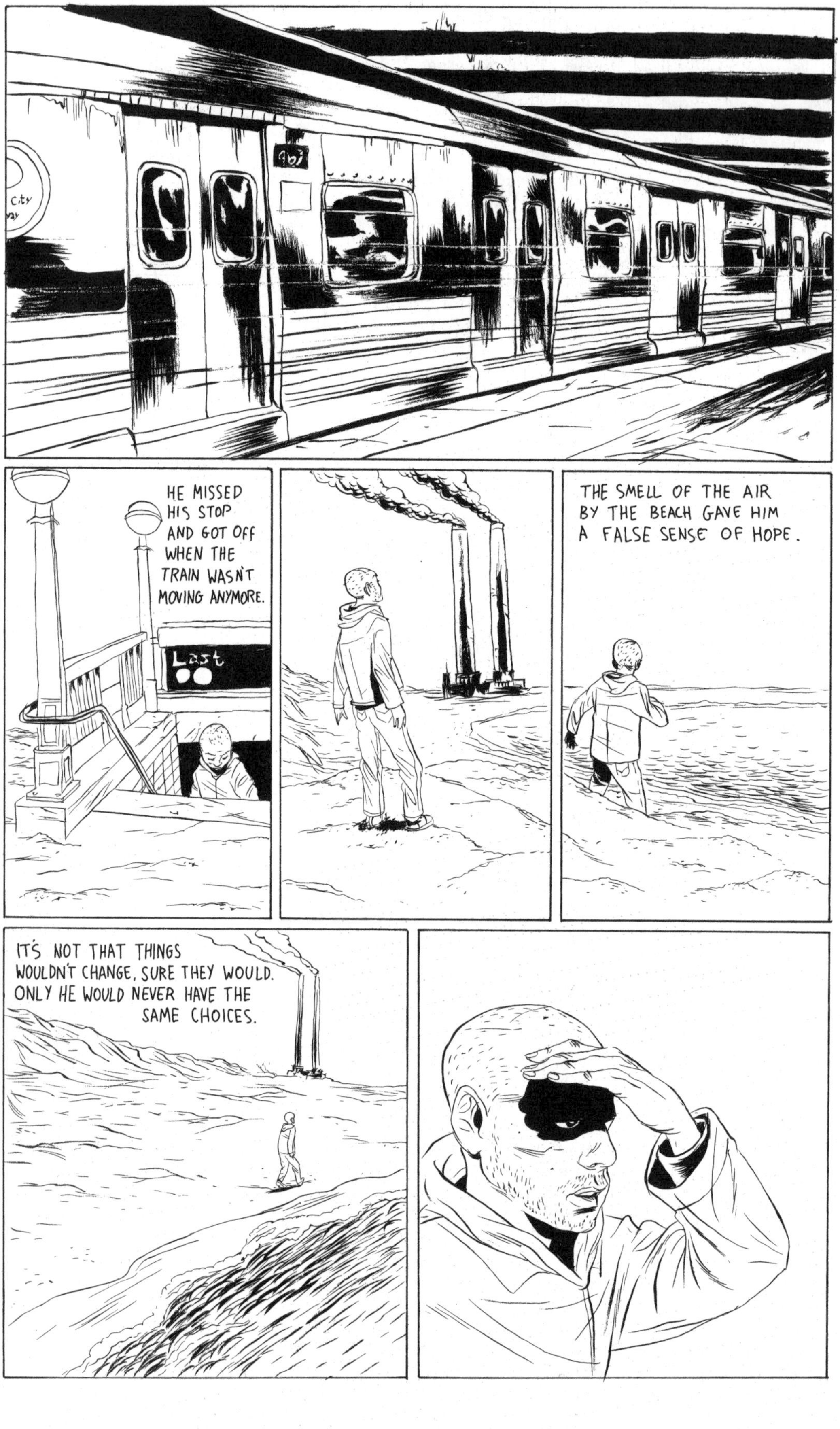
City
Last
HE MISSED HIS STOP AND GOT OFF WHEN THE TRAIN WASN'T MOVING ANYMORE.
THE SMELL OF THE AIR BY THE BEACH GAVE HIM A FALSE SENSE OF HOPE.
IT'S NOT THAT THINGS WOULDN'T CHANGE, SURE THEY WOULD. ONLY HE WOULD NEVER HAVE THE SAME CHOICES.

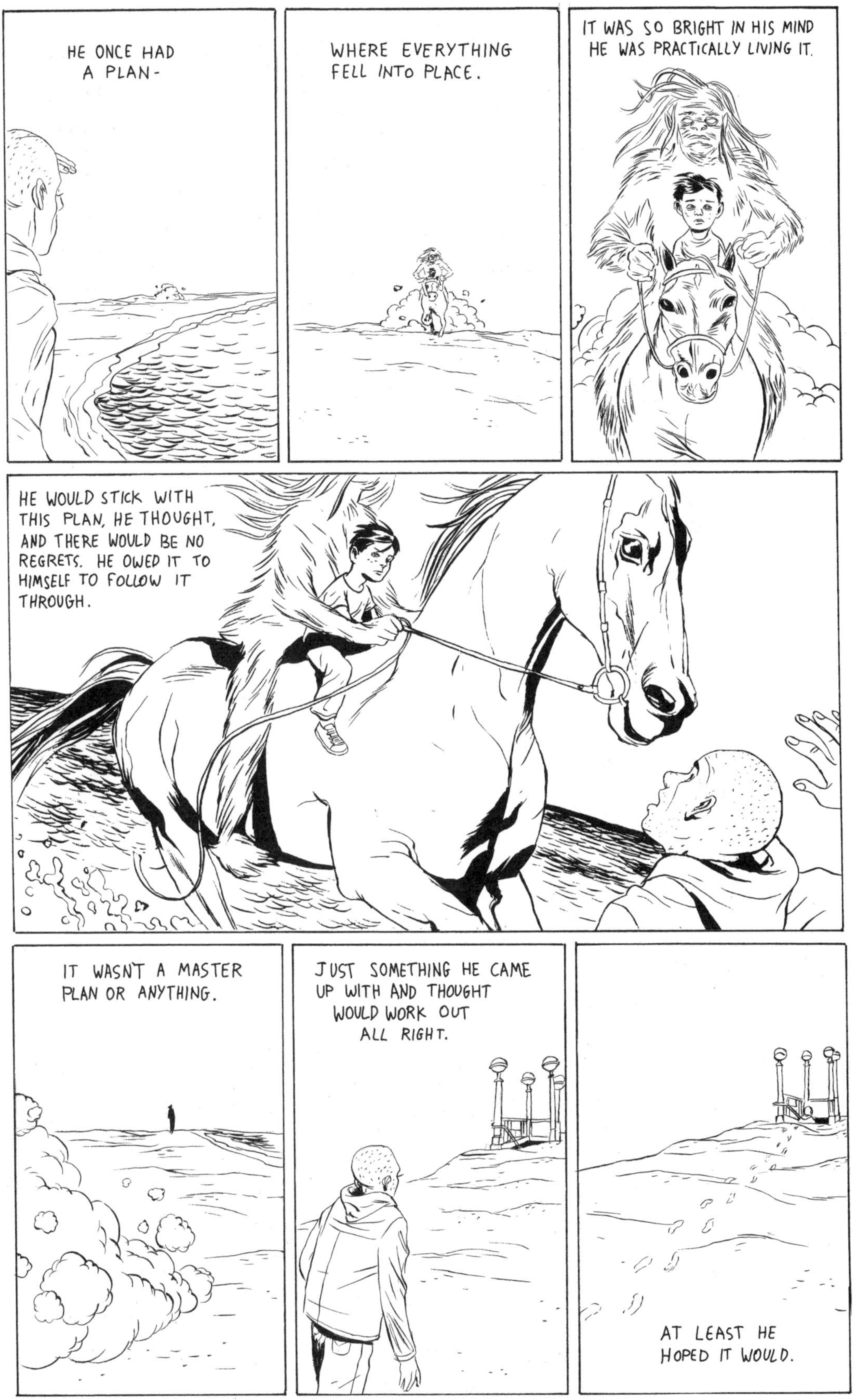
HE ONCE HAD A PLAN-
WHERE EVERYTHING FELL INTO PLACE.
IT WAS SO BRIGHT IN HIS MIND HE WAS PRACTICALLY LIVING IT.
HE WOULD STICK WITH THIS PLAN, HE THOUGHT, AND THERE WOULD BE NO REGRETS. HE OWED IT TO HIMSELF TO FOLLOW IT THROUGH.
IT WASN'T A MASTER PLAN OR ANYTHING.
JUST SOMETHING HE CAME UP WITH AND THOUGHT WOULD WORK OUT ALL RIGHT.
AT LEAST HE HOPED IT WOULD.

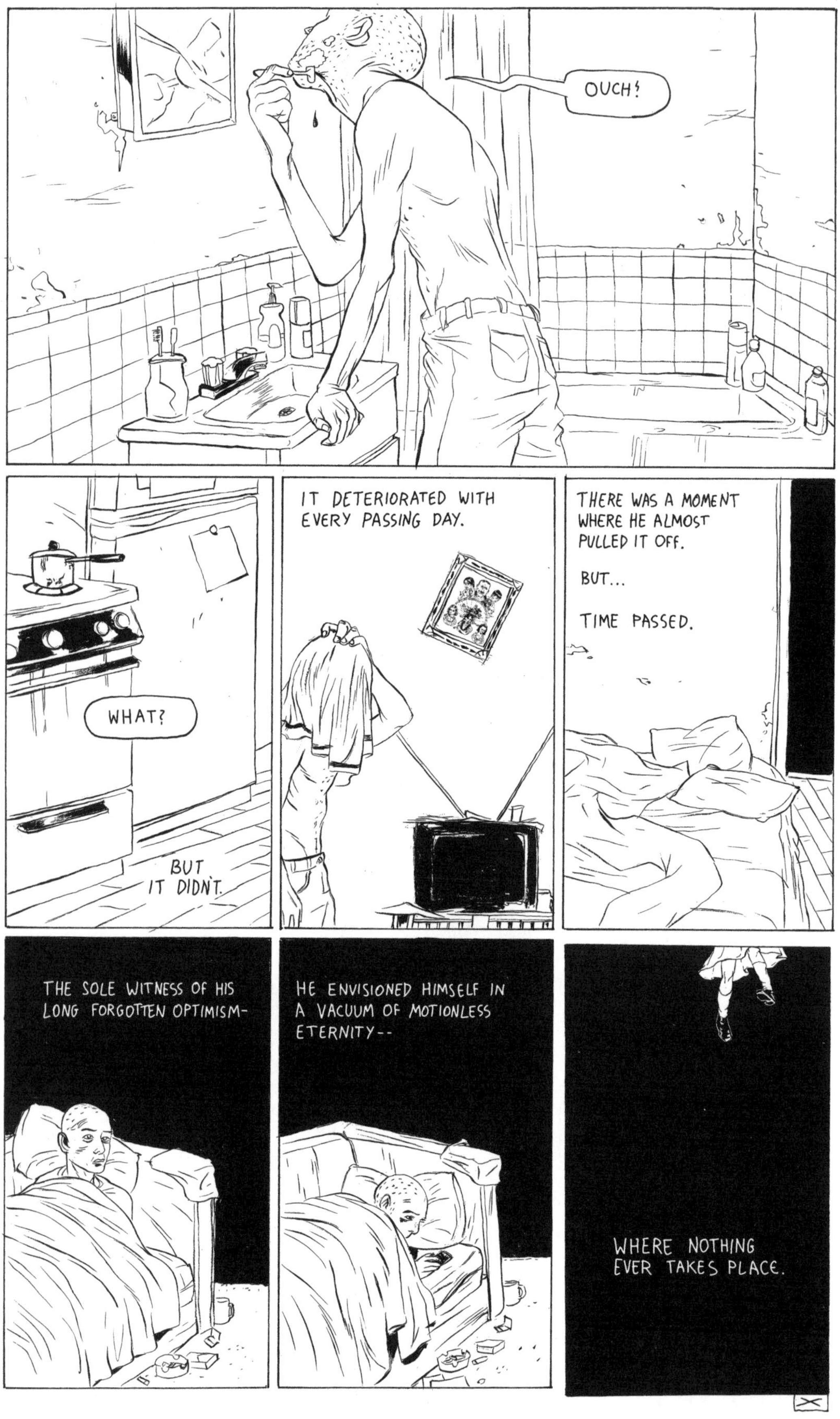
OUCH!
WHAT?
BUT IT DIDN'T.
IT DETERIORATED WITH EVERY PASSING DAY.
THERE WAS A MOMENT WHERE HE ALMOST PULLED IT OFF.
BUT...
TIME PASSED.
THE SOLE WITNESS OF HIS LONG FORGOTTEN OPTIMISM-
HE ENVISIONED HIMSELF IN A VACUUM OF MOTIONLESS ETERNITY--
WHERE NOTHING EVER TAKES PLACE.

Aquaflesh

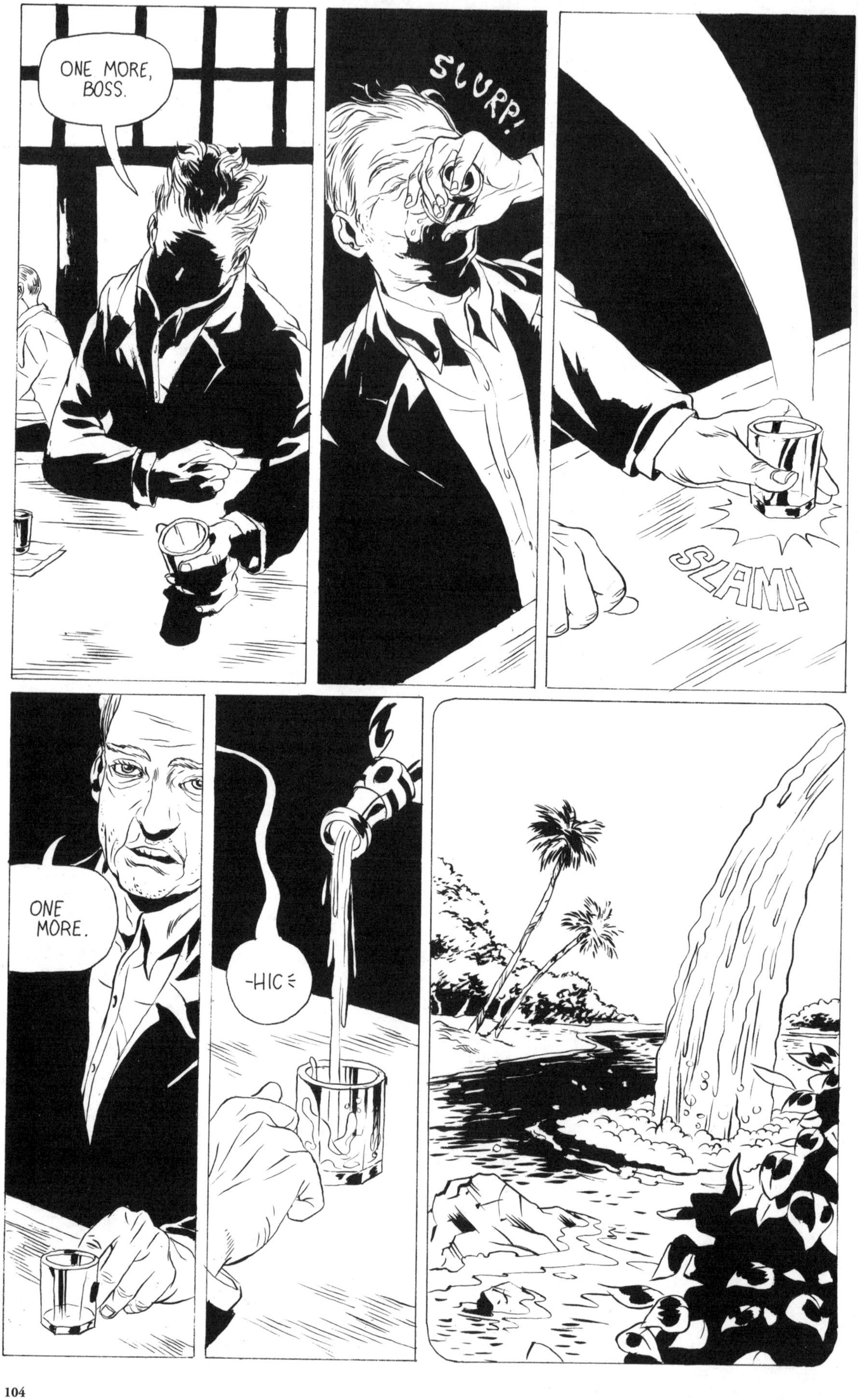
ONE MORE, BOSS.
SLURP!
SLAM!
ONE MORE.
-HIC

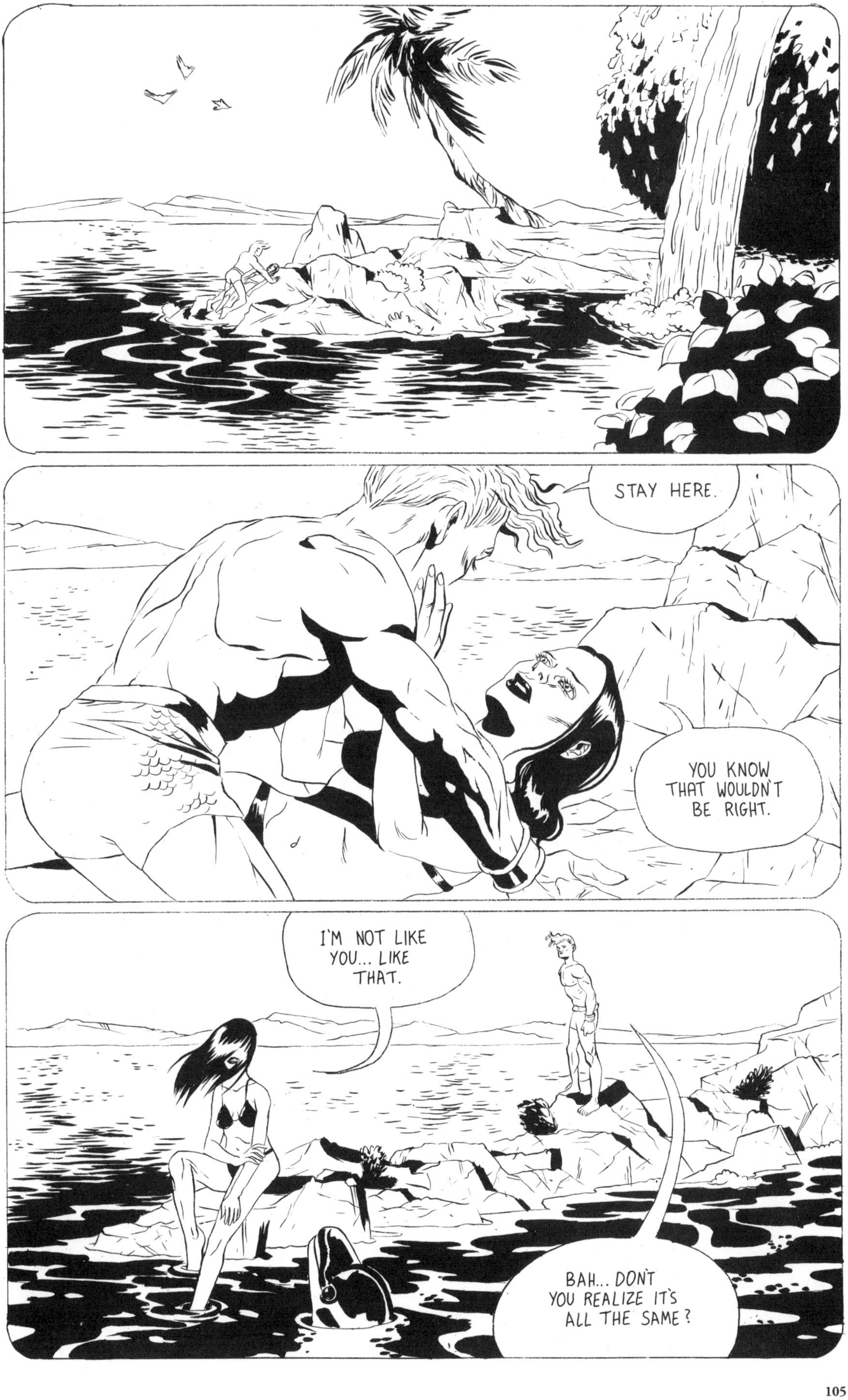
STAY HERE.
YOU KNOW THAT WOULDN'T BE RIGHT.
I'M NOT LIKE YOU... LIKE THAT.
BAH... DON'T YOU REALIZE IT'S ALL THE SAME?

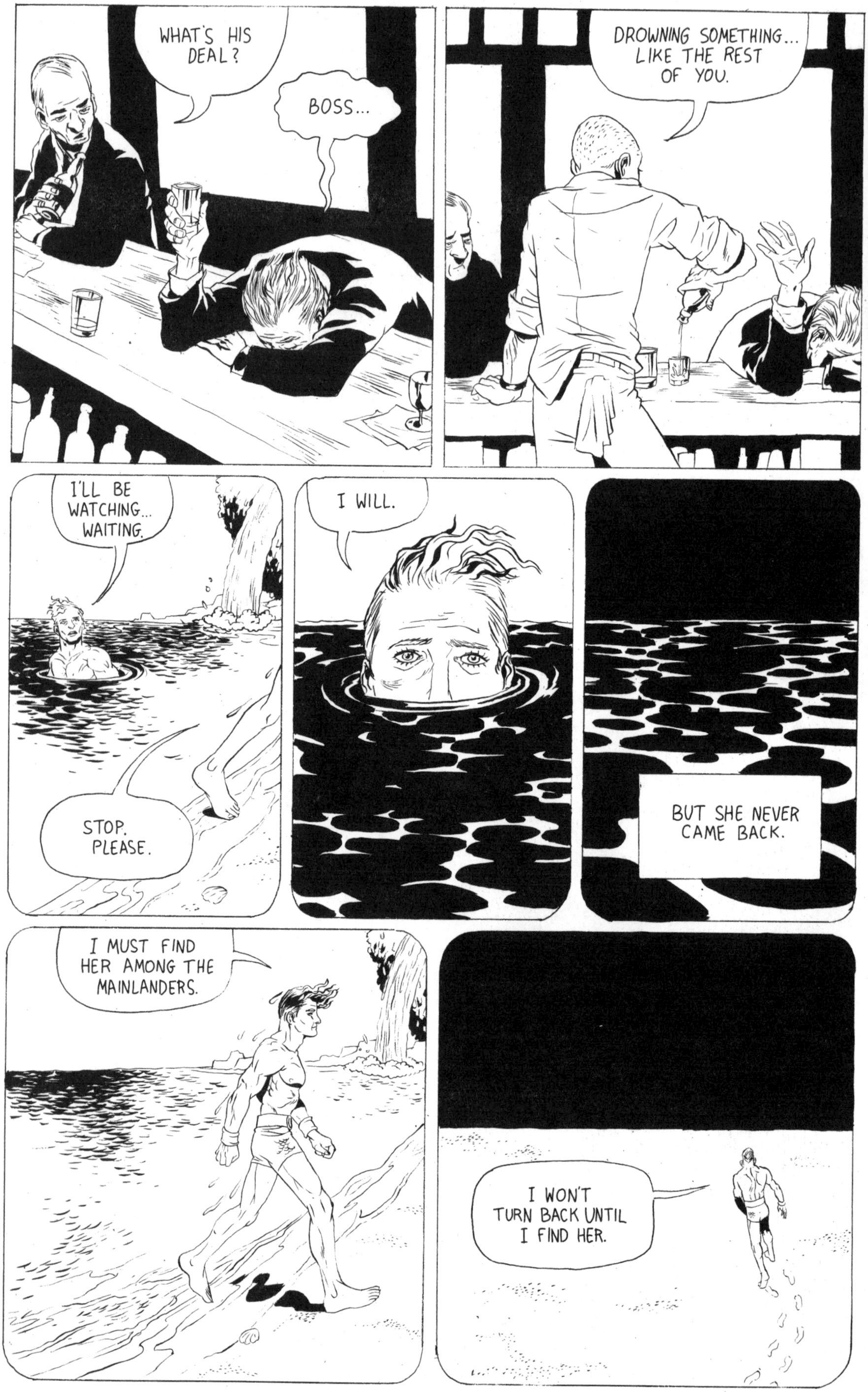
WHAT'S HIS DEAL?
BOSS...
DROWNING SOMETHING... LIKE THE REST OF YOU.
I'LL BE WATCHING... WAITING.
STOP. PLEASE.
I WILL.
BUT SHE NEVER CAME BACK.
I MUST FIND HER AMONG THE MAINLANDERS.
I WON'T TURN BACK UNTIL I FIND HER.

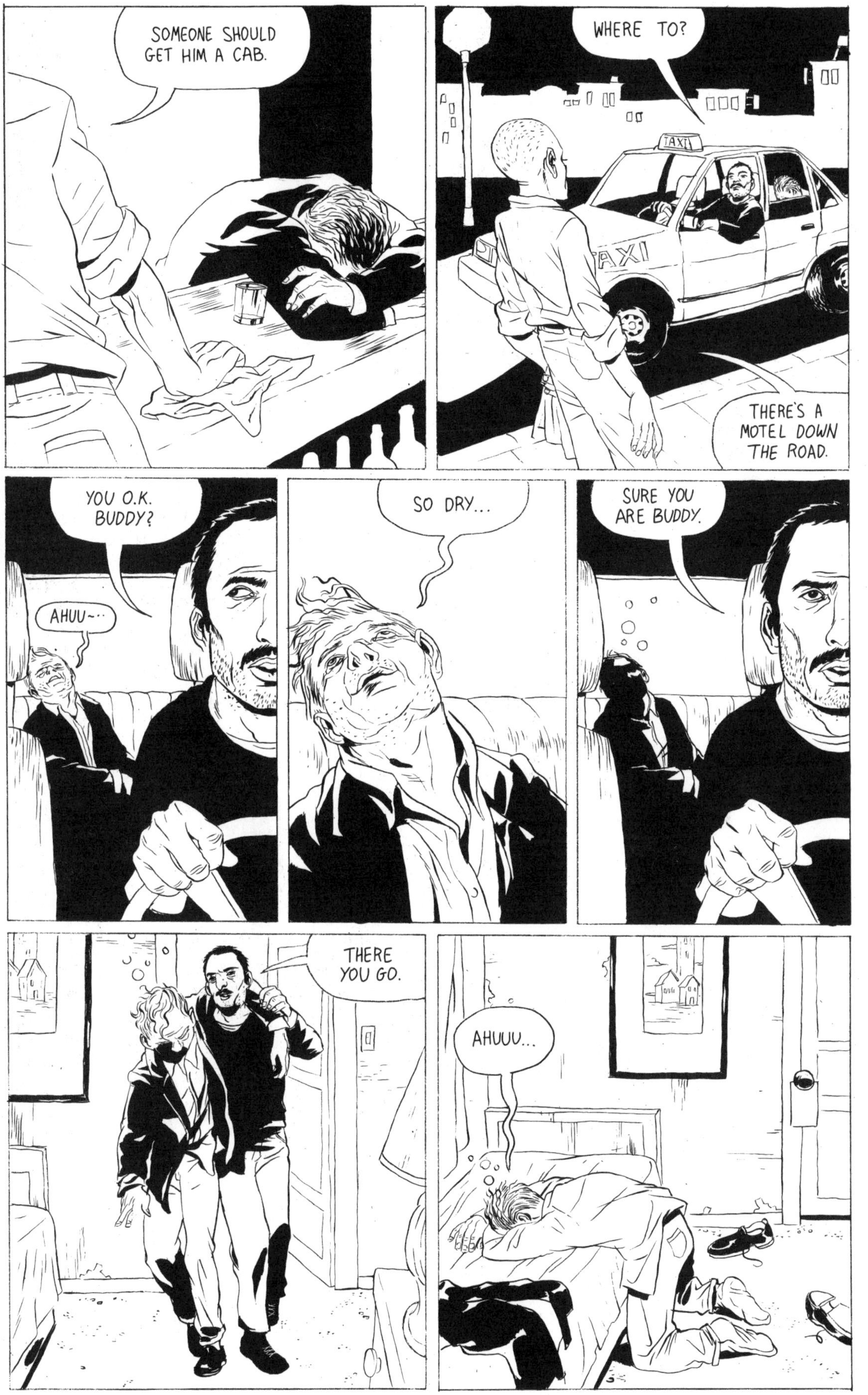
SOMEONE SHOULD GET HIM A CAB.
WHERE TO?
THERE'S A MOTEL DOWN THE ROAD.
YOU O.K. BUDDY?
AHUU~...
SO DRY...
SURE YOU ARE BUDDY.
THERE YOU GO.
AHUUU...

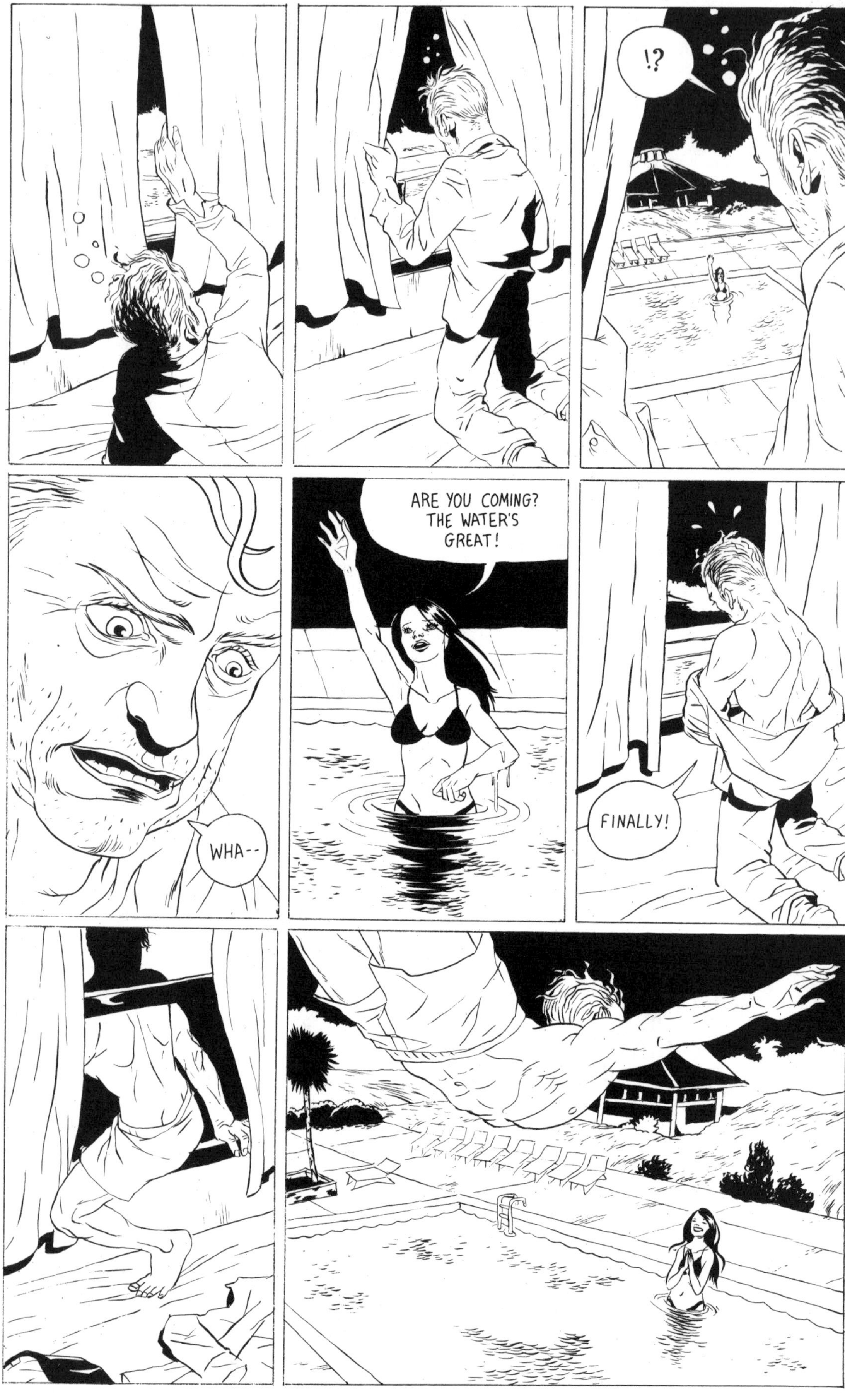
!?
WHA--
ARE YOU COMING? THE WATER'S GREAT!
FINALLY!

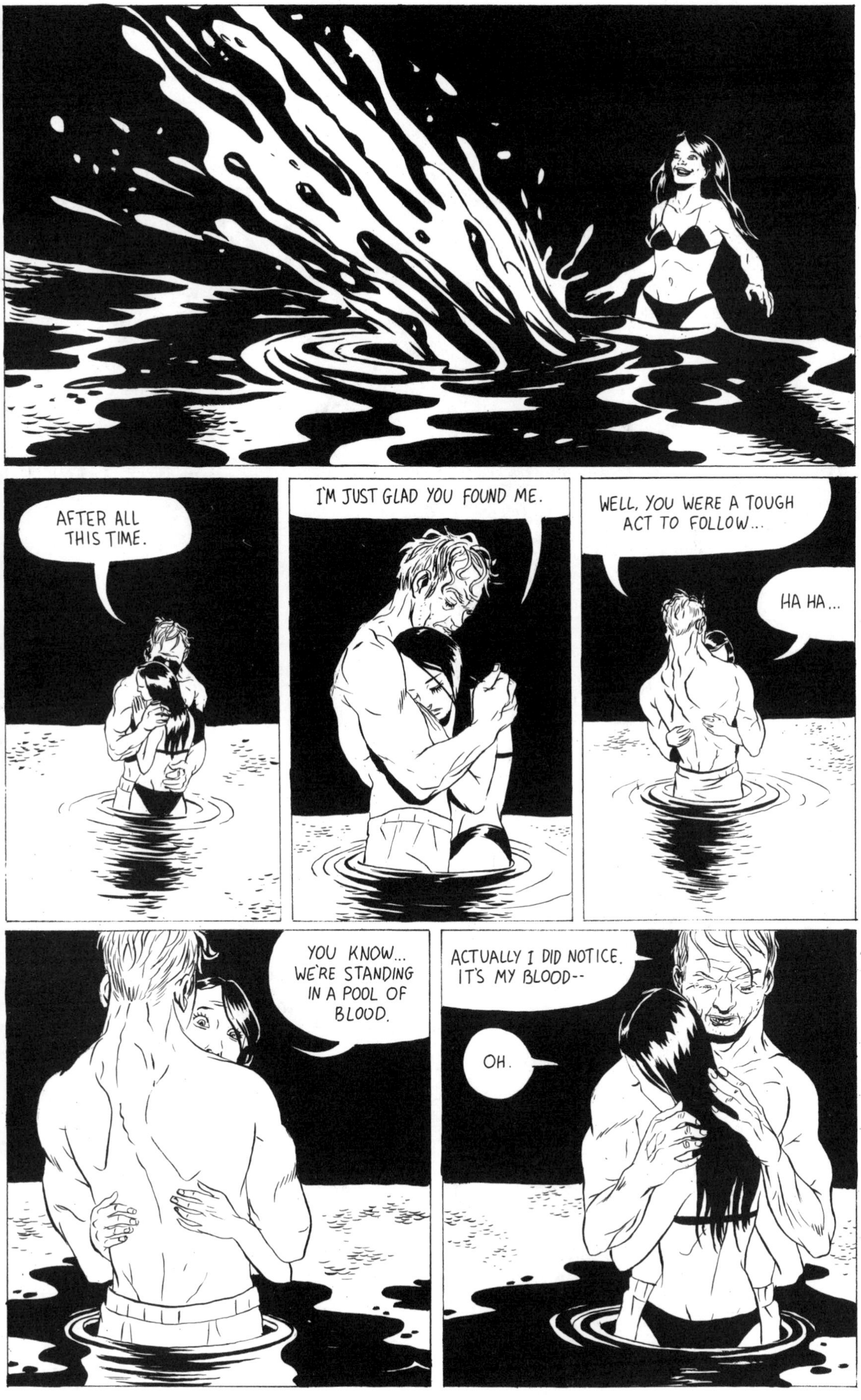

AFTER ALL THIS TIME.
I'M JUST GLAD YOU FOUND ME.
WELL, YOU WERE A TOUGH ACT TO FOLLOW...
HA HA...
YOU KNOW... WE'RE STANDING IN A POOL OF BLOOD.
ACTUALLY I DID NOTICE. IT'S MY BLOOD--
OH.

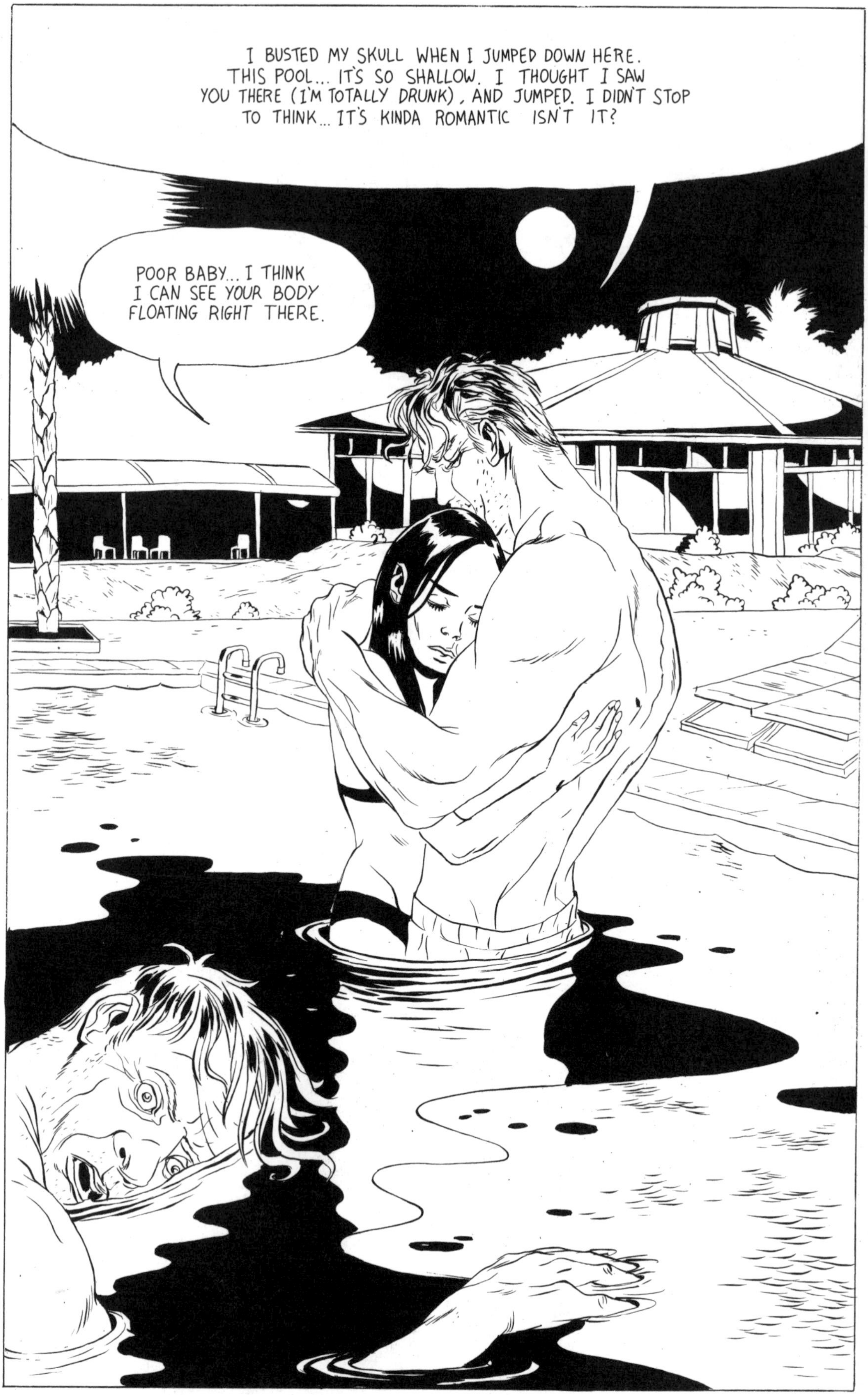
I BUSTED MY SKULL WHEN I JUMPED DOWN HERE. THIS POOL... IT'S SO SHALLOW. I THOUGHT I SAW YOU THERE (I'M TOTALLY DRUNK), AND JUMPED. I DIDN'T STOP TO THINK... IT'S KINDA ROMANTIC ISN'T IT?
POOR BABY... I THINK I CAN SEE YOUR BODY FLOATING RIGHT THERE.

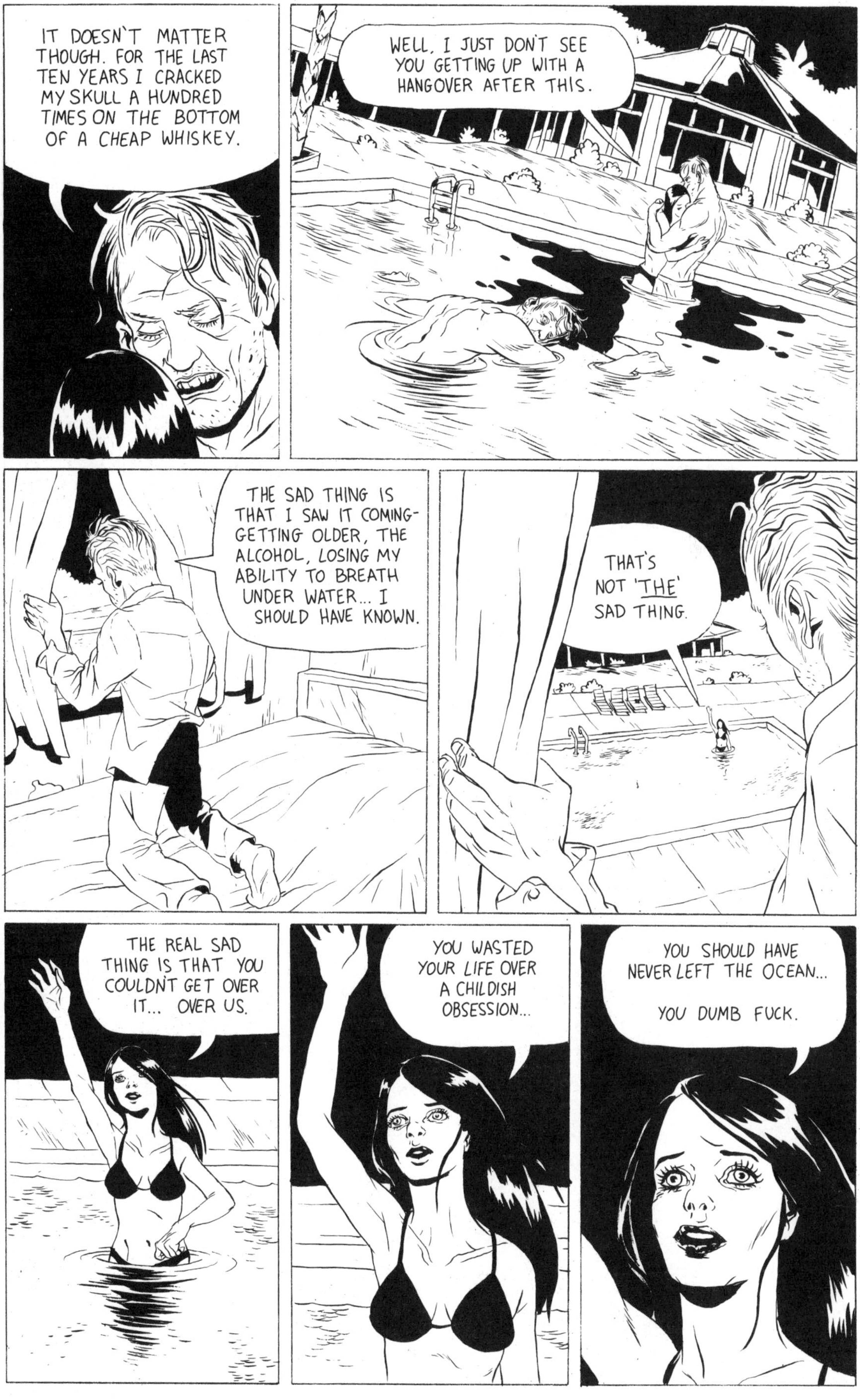
IT DOESN'T MATTER THOUGH. FOR THE LAST TEN YEARS I CRACKED MY SKULL A HUNDRED TIMES ON THE BOTTOM OF A CHEAP WHISKEY.
WELL, I JUST DON'T SEE YOU GETTING UP WITH A HANGOVER AFTER THIS.
THE SAD THING IS THAT I SAW IT COMING-GETTING OLDER, THE ALCOHOL, LOSING MY ABILITY TO BREATH UNDER WATER... I SHOULD HAVE KNOWN.
THAT'S NOT 'THE' SAD THING.
THE REAL SAD THING IS THAT YOU COULDN'T GET OVER IT... OVER US.
YOU WASTED YOUR LIFE OVER A CHILDISH OBSESSION...
YOU SHOULD HAVE NEVER LEFT THE OCEAN...
YOU DUMB FUCK.

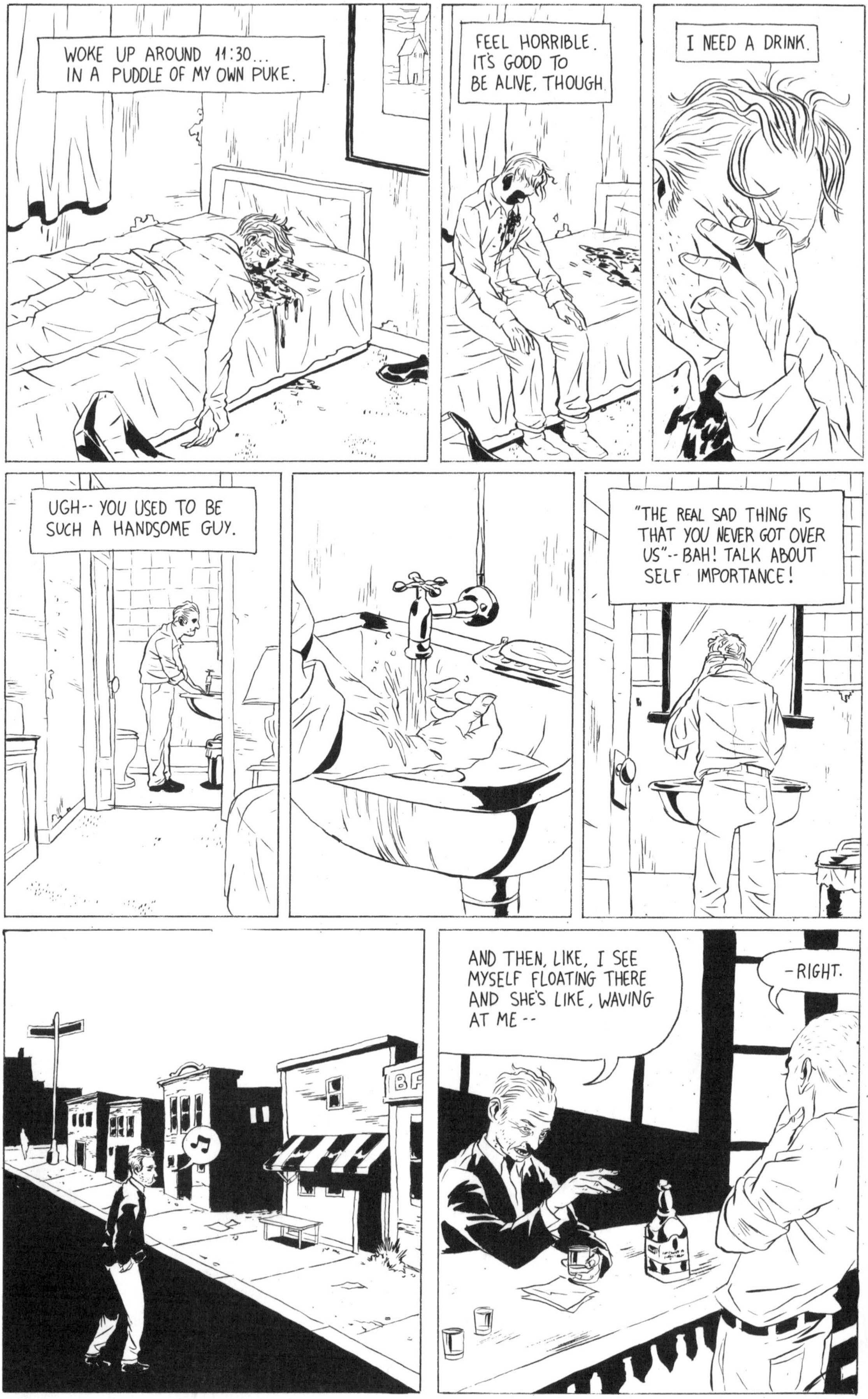

WOKE UP AROUND 11:30... IN A PUDDLE OF MY OWN PUKE.
FEEL HORRIBLE. IT'S GOOD TO BE ALIVE, THOUGH.
I NEED A DRINK.
UGH-- YOU USED TO BE SUCH A HANDSOME GUY.
"THE REAL SAD THING IS THAT YOU NEVER GOT OVER US"-- BAH! TALK ABOUT SELF IMPORTANCE!
AND THEN, LIKE, I SEE MYSELF FLOATING THERE AND SHE'S LIKE, WAVING AT ME --
-RIGHT.

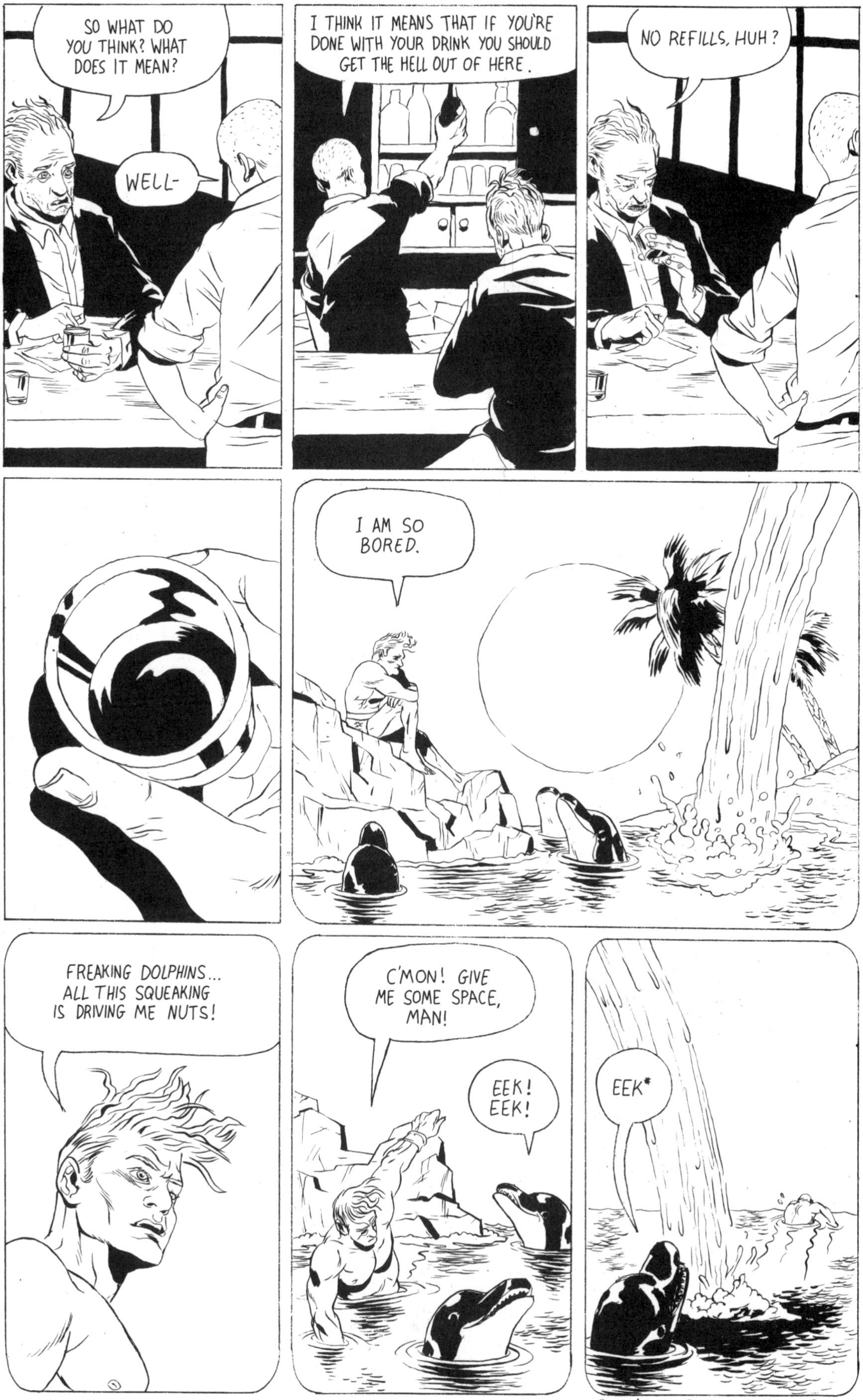
SO WHAT DO YOU THINK? WHAT DOES IT MEAN?
WELL-
I THINK IT MEANS THAT IF YOU'RE DONE WITH YOUR DRINK YOU SHOULD GET THE HELL OUT OF HERE.
NO REFILLS, HUH?
I AM SO BORED.
FREAKING DOLPHINS... ALL THIS SQUEAKING IS DRIVING ME NUTS!
C'MON! GIVE ME SOME SPACE, MAN!
EEK! EEK!
EEK*

*DON'T GO THERE, NOBODY GOES OVER TO THAT SIDE.

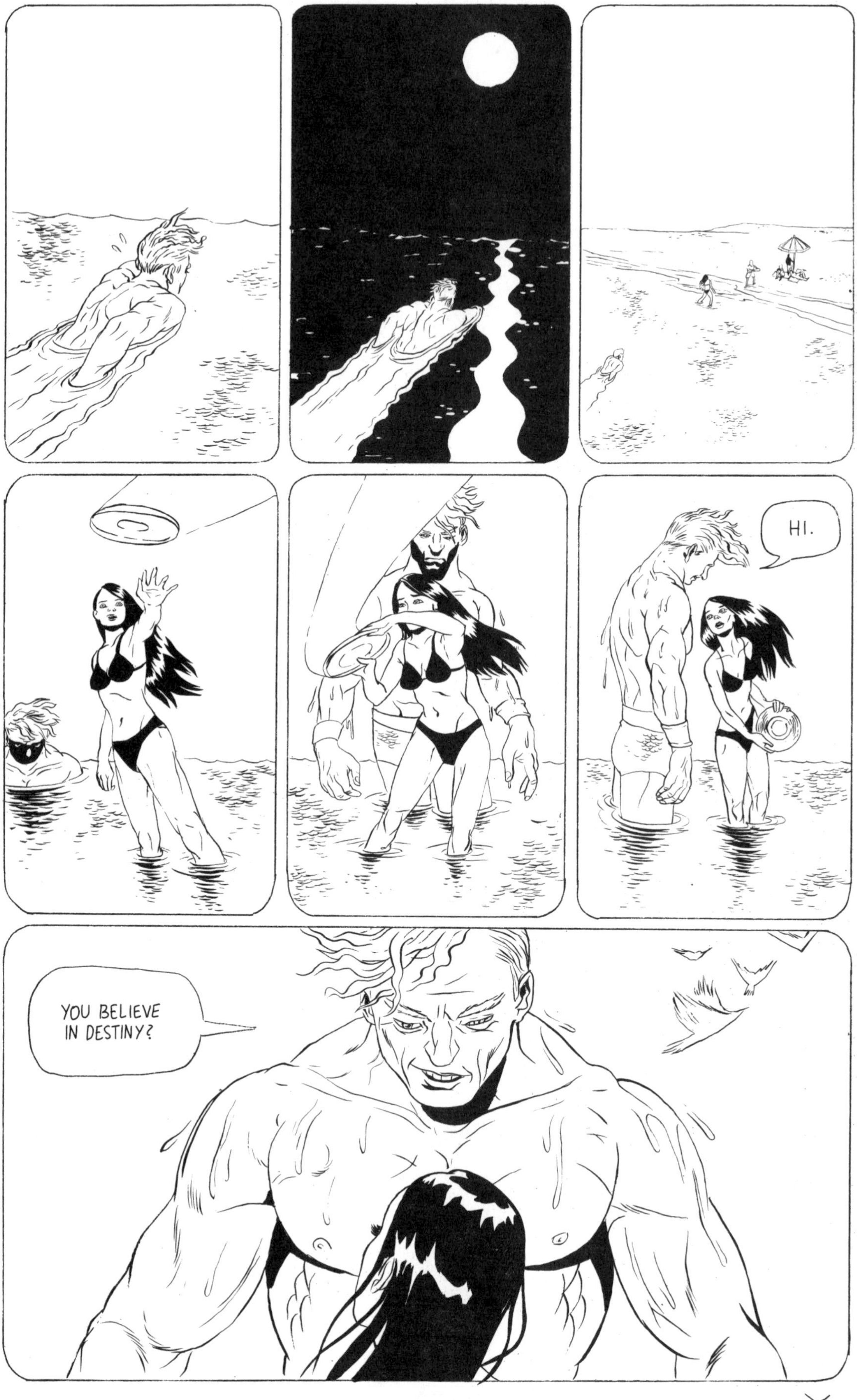
HI.
YOU BELIEVE IN DESTINY?

Morocco

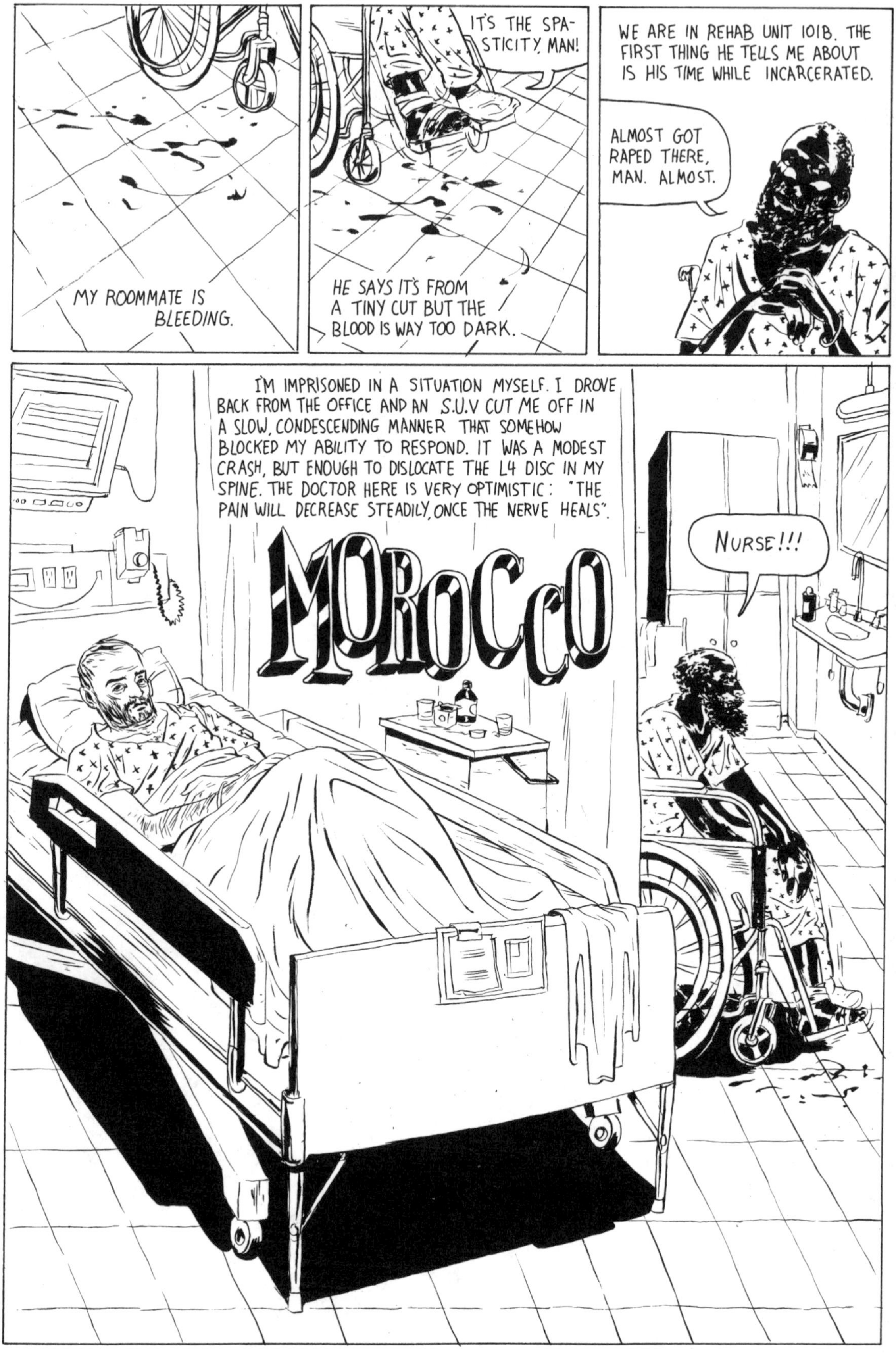
MY ROOMMATE IS BLEEDING.
IT'S THE SPA-STICITY, MAN!
HE SAYS IT'S FROM A TINY CUT BUT THE BLOOD IS WAY TOO DARK.
WE ARE IN REHAB UNIT 101B. THE FIRST THING HE TELLS ME ABOUT IS HIS TIME WHILE INCARCERATED.
ALMOST GOT RAPED THERE, MAN. ALMOST.
I'M IMPRISONED IN A SITUATION MYSELF. I DROVE BACK FROM THE OFFICE AND AN S.U.V CUT ME OFF IN A SLOW, CONDESCENDING MANNER THAT SOMEHOW BLOCKED MY ABILITY TO RESPOND. IT WAS A MODEST CRASH, BUT ENOUGH TO DISLOCATE THE L4 DISC IN MY SPINE. THE DOCTOR HERE IS VERY OPTIMISTIC: "THE PAIN WILL DECREASE STEADILY, ONCE THE NERVE HEALS".
MOROCCO
NURSE!!!

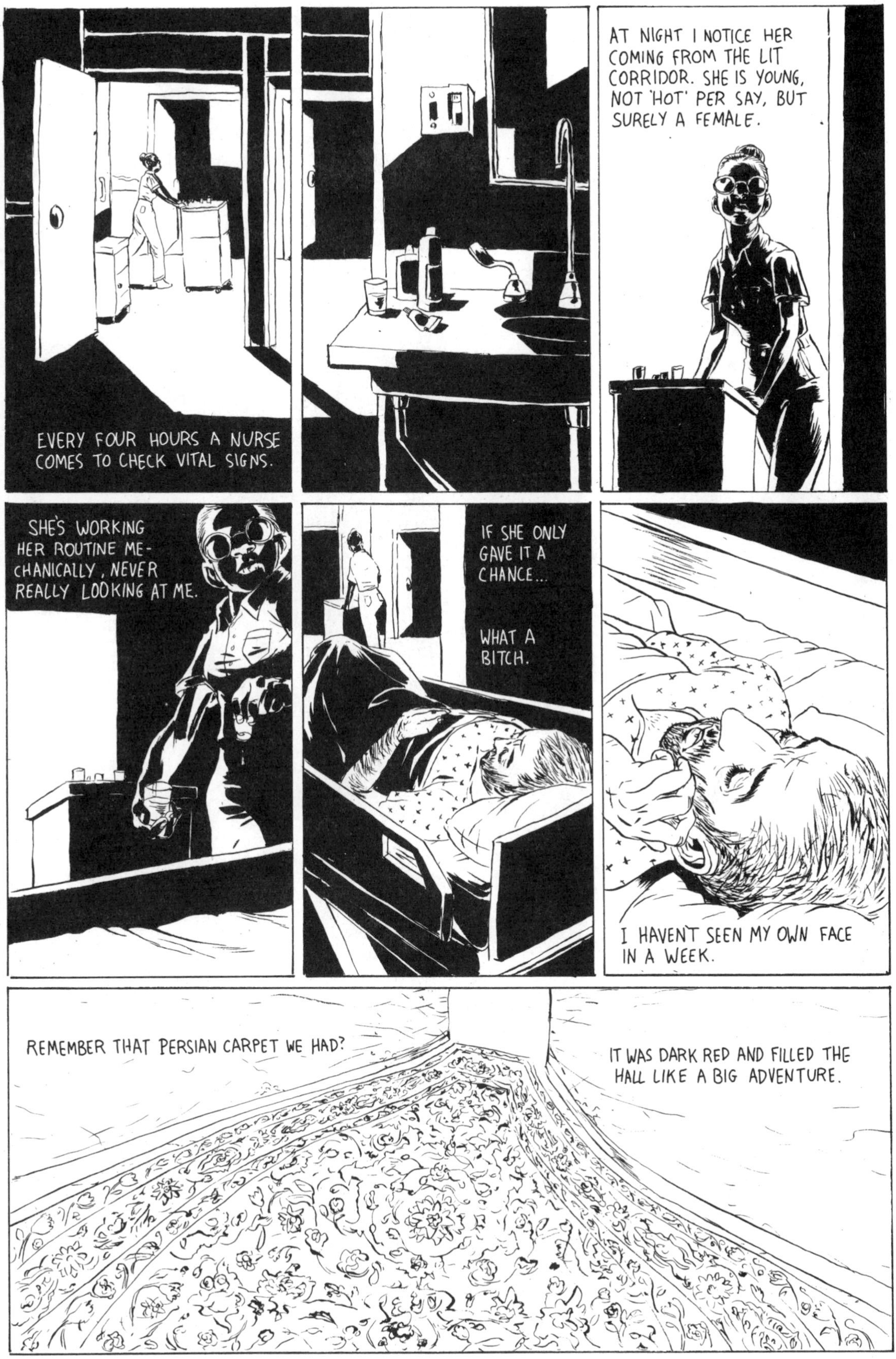
EVERY FOUR HOURS A NURSE COMES TO CHECK VITAL SIGNS.
AT NIGHT I NOTICE HER COMING FROM THE LIT CORRIDOR. SHE IS YOUNG, NOT 'HOT' PER SAY, BUT SURELY A FEMALE.
SHE'S WORKING HER ROUTINE MECHANICALLY, NEVER REALLY LOOKING AT ME.
IF SHE ONLY GAVE IT A CHANCE...
WHAT A BITCH.
I HAVEN'T SEEN MY OWN FACE IN A WEEK.
REMEMBER THAT PERSIAN CARPET WE HAD?
IT WAS DARK RED AND FILLED THE HALL LIKE A BIG ADVENTURE.

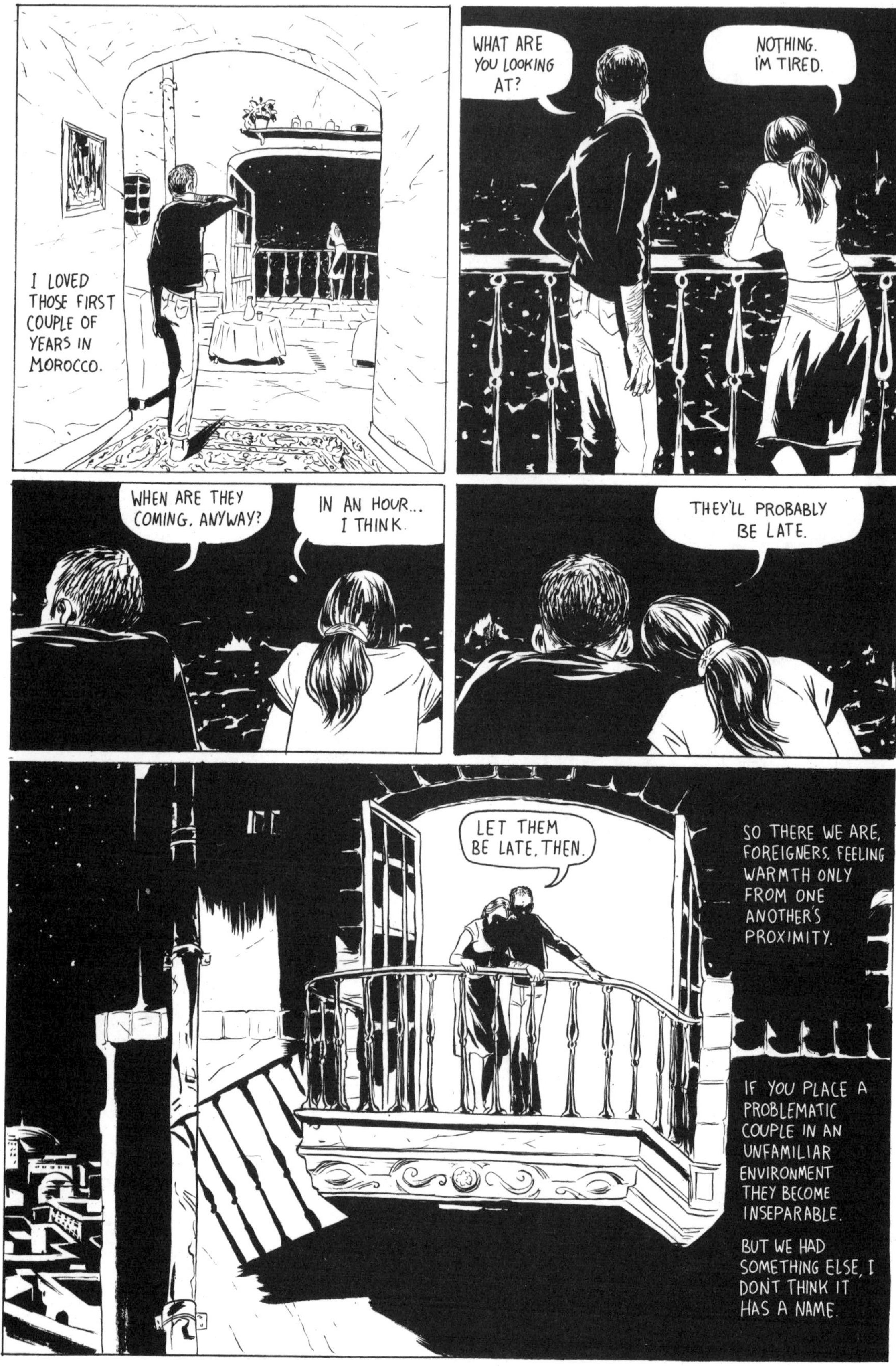
I LOVED THOSE FIRST COUPLE OF YEARS IN MOROCCO.
WHAT ARE YOU LOOKING AT?
NOTHING. I'M TIRED.
WHEN ARE THEY COMING, ANYWAY?
IN AN HOUR... I THINK.
THEY'LL PROBABLY BE LATE.
LET THEM BE LATE, THEN.
SO THERE WE ARE, FOREIGNERS, FEELING WARMTH ONLY FROM ONE ANOTHER'S PROXIMITY.
IF YOU PLACE A PROBLEMATIC COUPLE IN AN UNFAMILIAR ENVIRONMENT THEY BECOME INSEPARABLE.
BUT WE HAD SOMETHING ELSE, I DON'T THINK IT HAS A NAME.

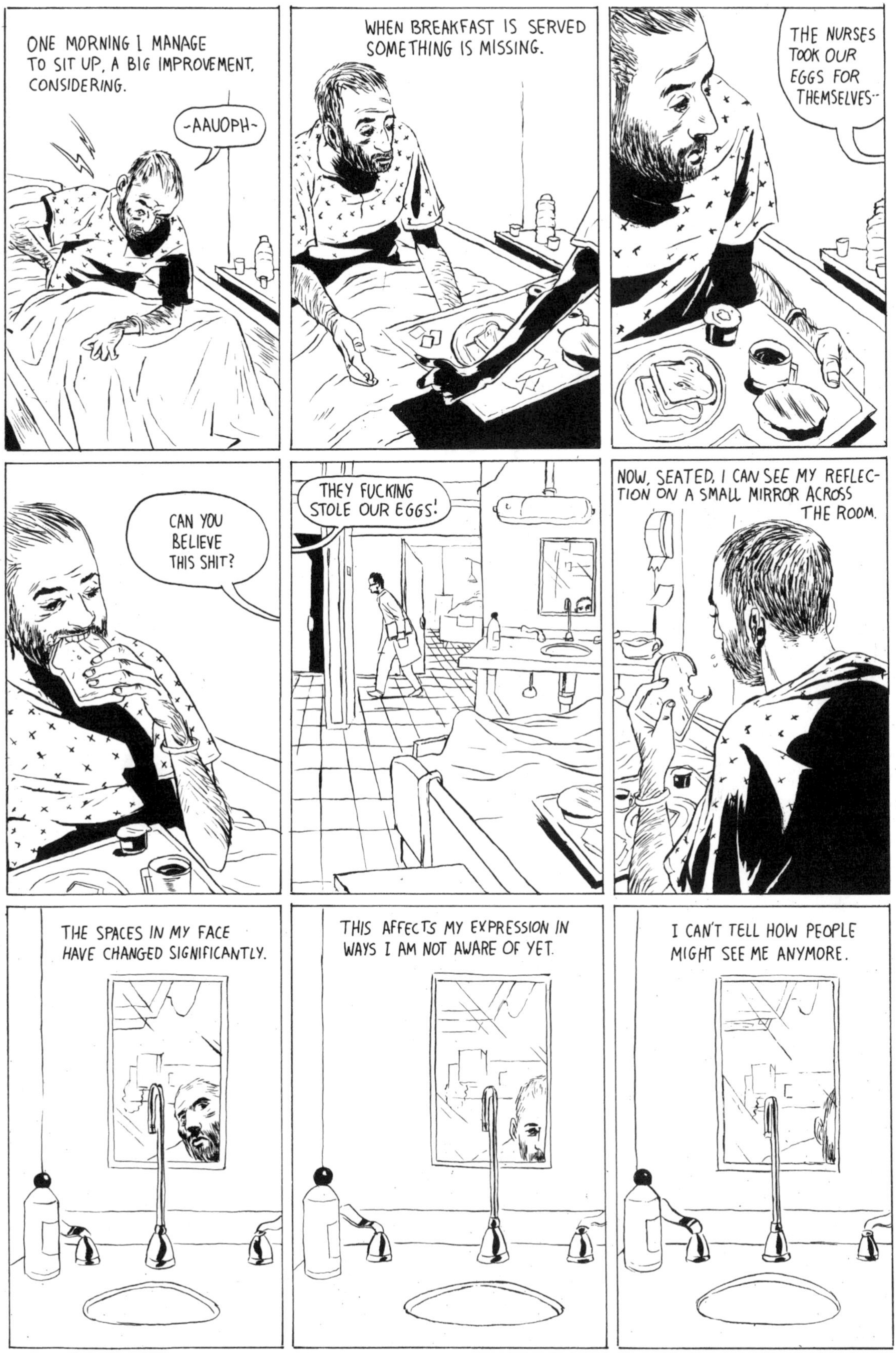
ONE MORNING I MANAGE TO SIT UP, A BIG IMPROVEMENT, CONSIDERING.
-AAUOPH-
WHEN BREAKFAST IS SERVED SOMETHING IS MISSING.
THE NURSES TOOK OUR EGGS FOR THEMSELVES--
CAN YOU BELIEVE THIS SHIT?
THEY FUCKING STOLE OUR EGGS!
NOW, SEATED, I CAN SEE MY REFLECTION ON A SMALL MIRROR ACROSS THE ROOM.
THE SPACES IN MY FACE HAVE CHANGED SIGNIFICANTLY.
THIS AFFECTS MY EXPRESSION IN WAYS I AM NOT AWARE OF YET.
I CAN'T TELL HOW PEOPLE MIGHT SEE ME ANYMORE.

YOUR FRIENDS CAME OVER (OR WERE THEY FRIENDS OF FRIENDS?) TOPIC DISCUSSED: PHYSICAL VS. EMOTIONAL PAIN—WHICH IS BETTER?

YOUR CHEEKS RED WITH WINE—

WHY ARE THEY STAYING FOR SO LONG?

YOU WERE DOING SOMETHING IN THE KITCHEN...

AND A FRIEND OF YOURS- WHAT'S HIS NAME - TOLD ME ABOUT A NEW IMMIGRATION POLICY.

IT TURNS OUT HE WORKS FOR THE GOVERNMENT.

IT TURNS OUT THEY'VE DEVELOPED A NEW WAY OF TRACKING DOWN ILLEGAL IMMIGRANTS.

"THE FACIAL HAIR LINE, THE 'SHAVE LINE'" HE TELLS ME. "NOTICE THE CHANGING CURVE".
A. IMMIGRANT.
B. NONIMMIGRANT.

A.

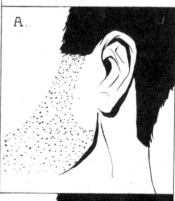

B.

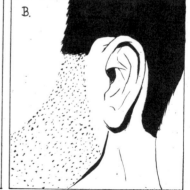

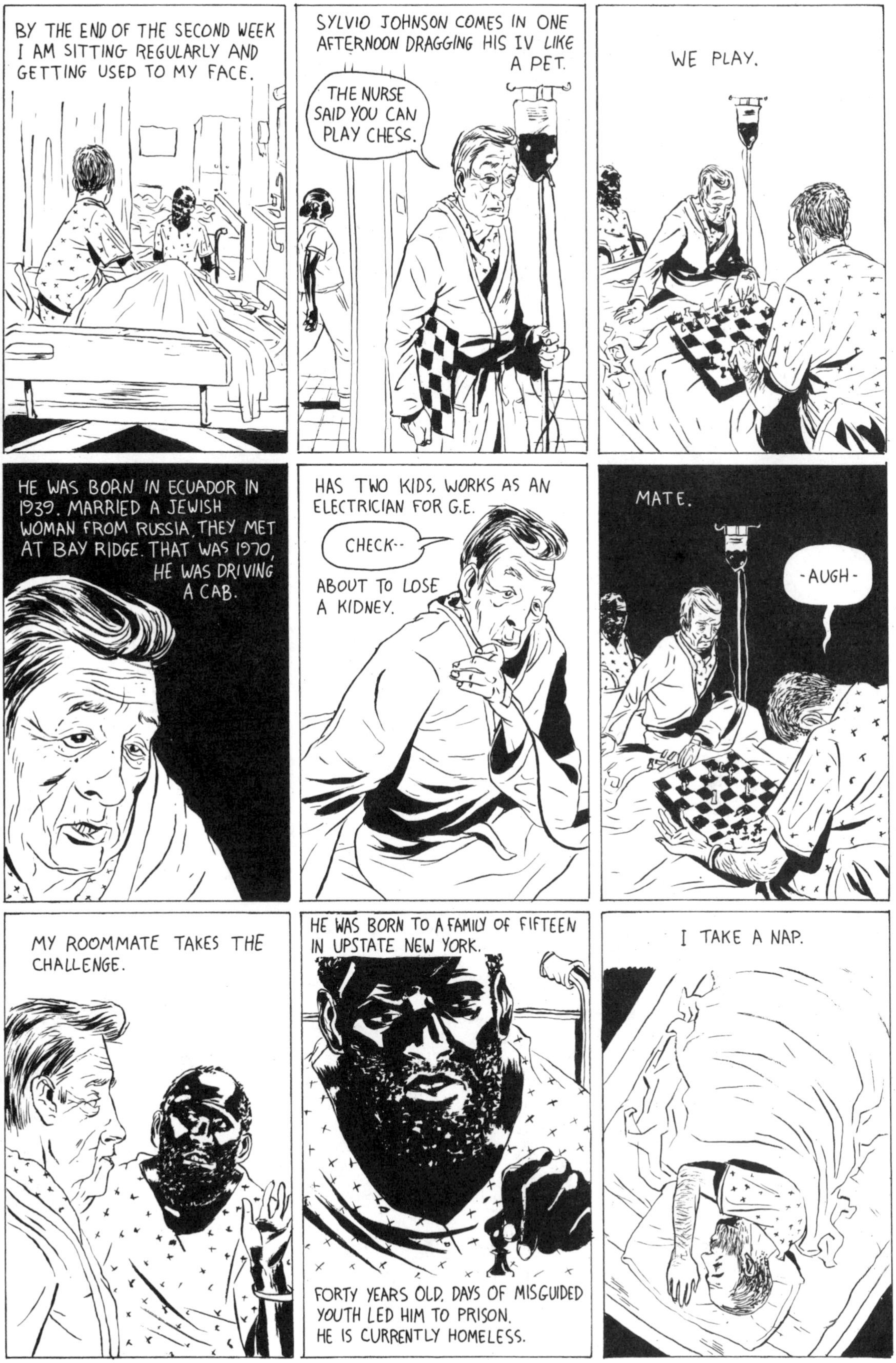
BY THE END OF THE SECOND WEEK I AM SITTING REGULARLY AND GETTING USED TO MY FACE.
SYLVIO JOHNSON COMES IN ONE AFTERNOON DRAGGING HIS IV LIKE A PET.
THE NURSE SAID YOU CAN PLAY CHESS.
WE PLAY.
HE WAS BORN IN ECUADOR IN 1939. MARRIED A JEWISH WOMAN FROM RUSSIA, THEY MET AT BAY RIDGE. THAT WAS 1970, HE WAS DRIVING A CAB.
HAS TWO KIDS, WORKS AS AN ELECTRICIAN FOR G.E.
CHECK--
ABOUT TO LOSE A KIDNEY.
MATE.
-AUGH-
MY ROOMMATE TAKES THE CHALLENGE.
HE WAS BORN TO A FAMILY OF FIFTEEN IN UPSTATE NEW YORK.
FORTY YEARS OLD. DAYS OF MISGUIDED YOUTH LED HIM TO PRISON. HE IS CURRENTLY HOMELESS.
I TAKE A NAP.

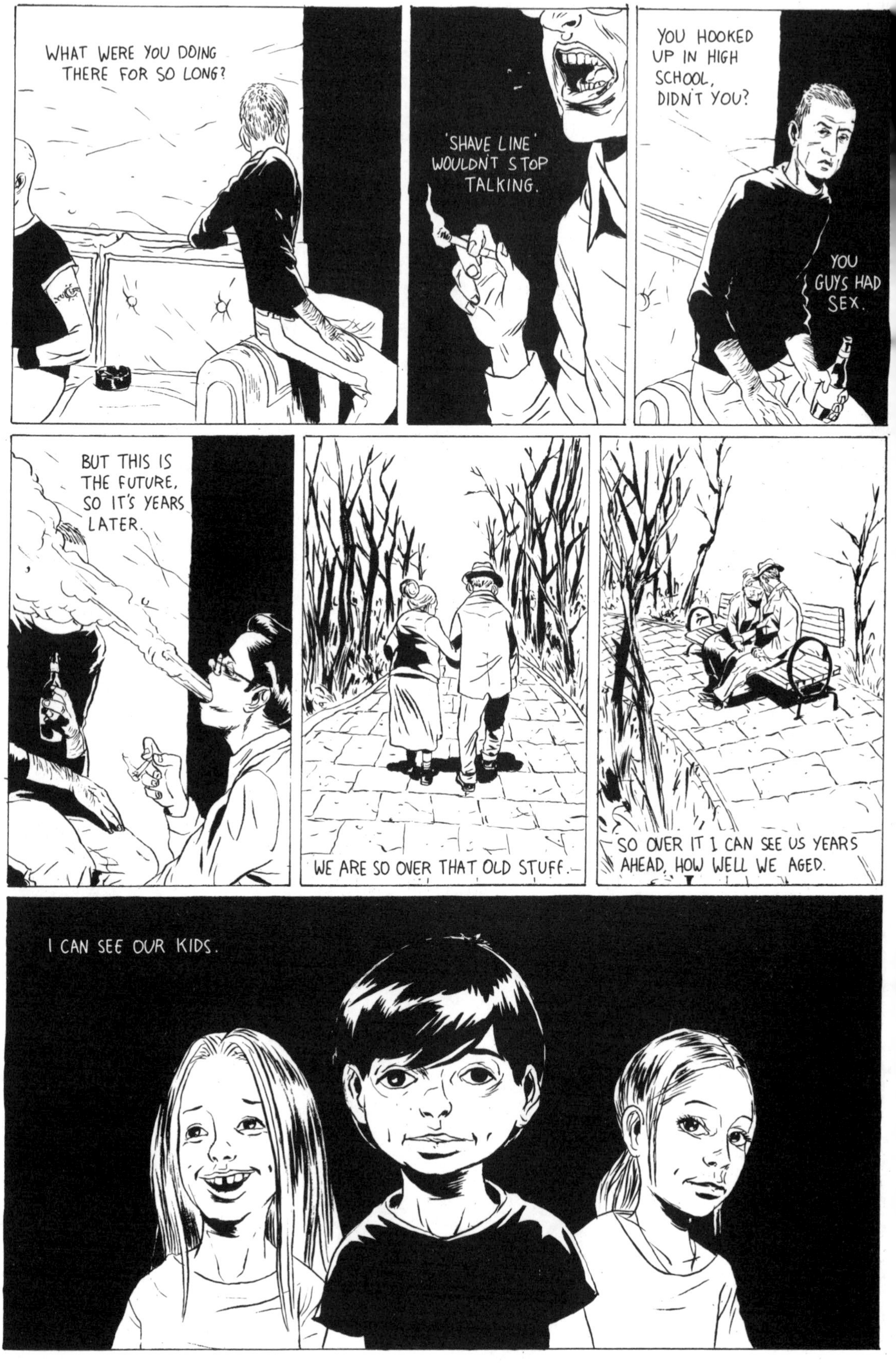
WHAT WERE YOU DOING THERE FOR SO LONG?
'SHAVE LINE' WOULDN'T STOP TALKING.
YOU HOOKED UP IN HIGH SCHOOL, DIDN'T YOU?
YOU GUYS HAD SEX.
BUT THIS IS THE FUTURE, SO IT'S YEARS LATER.
WE ARE SO OVER THAT OLD STUFF.
SO OVER IT I CAN SEE US YEARS AHEAD, HOW WELL WE AGED.
I CAN SEE OUR KIDS.

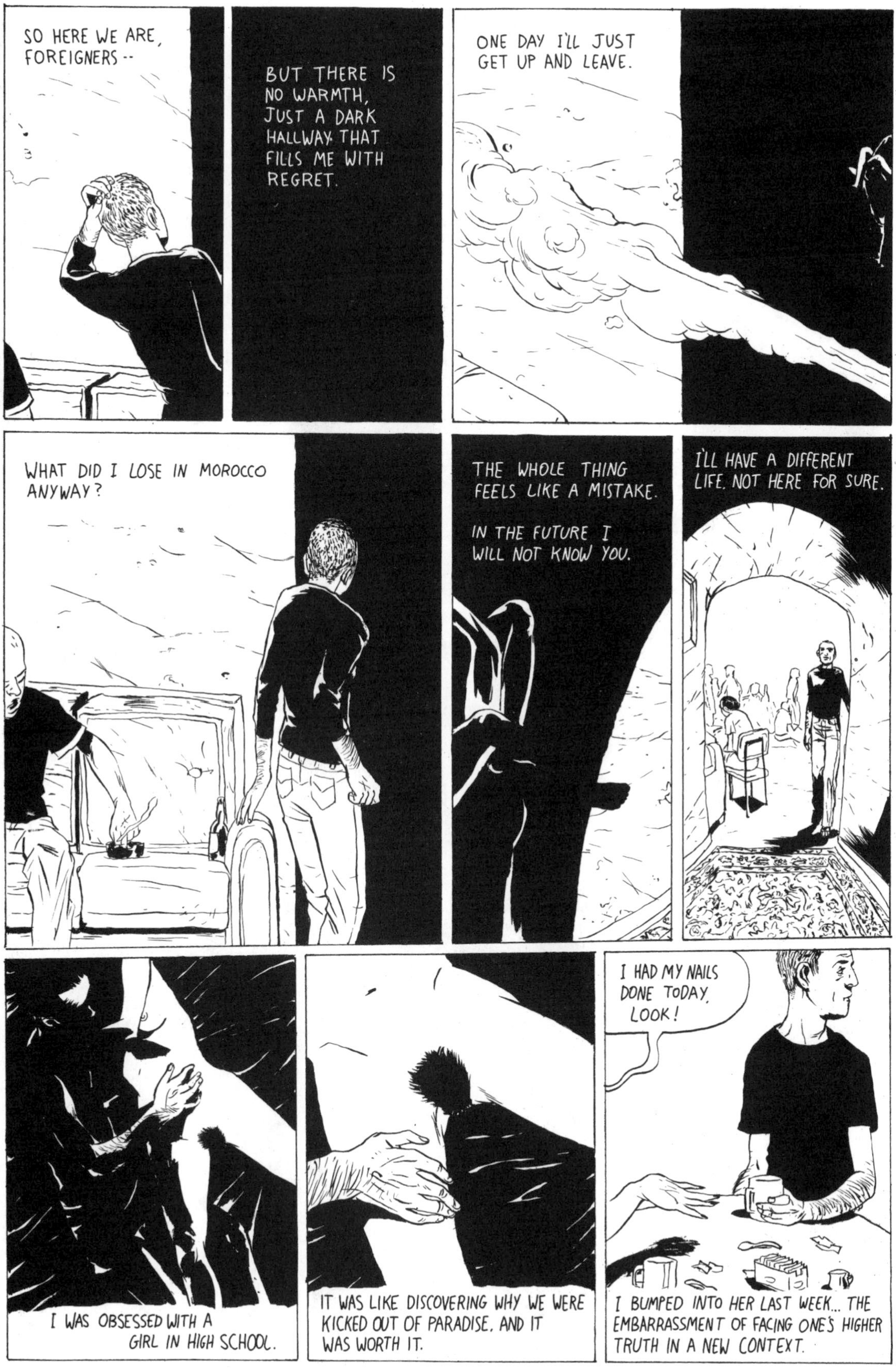
SO HERE WE ARE, FOREIGNERS --
BUT THERE IS NO WARMTH, JUST A DARK HALLWAY THAT FILLS ME WITH REGRET.
ONE DAY I'LL JUST GET UP AND LEAVE.
WHAT DID I LOSE IN MOROCCO ANYWAY?
THE WHOLE THING FEELS LIKE A MISTAKE.
IN THE FUTURE I WILL NOT KNOW YOU.
I'LL HAVE A DIFFERENT LIFE. NOT HERE FOR SURE.
I WAS OBSESSED WITH A GIRL IN HIGH SCHOOL.
IT WAS LIKE DISCOVERING WHY WE WERE KICKED OUT OF PARADISE, AND IT WAS WORTH IT.
I HAD MY NAILS DONE TODAY, LOOK!
I BUMPED INTO HER LAST WEEK... THE EMBARRASSMENT OF FACING ONE'S HIGHER TRUTH IN A NEW CONTEXT.

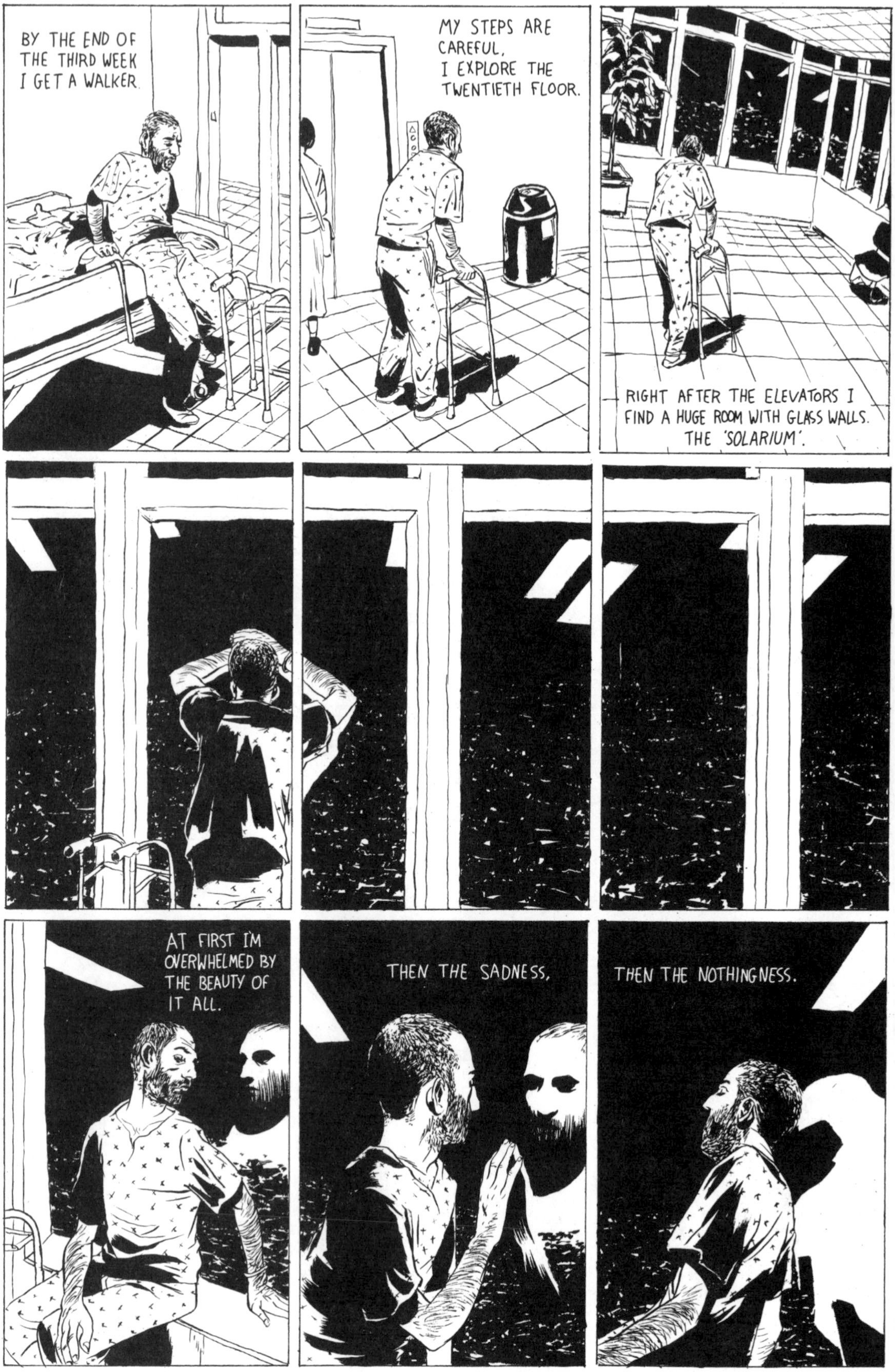
BY THE END OF THE THIRD WEEK I GET A WALKER.
MY STEPS ARE CAREFUL, I EXPLORE THE TWENTIETH FLOOR.
RIGHT AFTER THE ELEVATORS I FIND A HUGE ROOM WITH GLASS WALLS. THE 'SOLARIUM'.
AT FIRST I'M OVERWHELMED BY THE BEAUTY OF IT ALL.
THEN THE SADNESS,
THEN THE NOTHINGNESS.

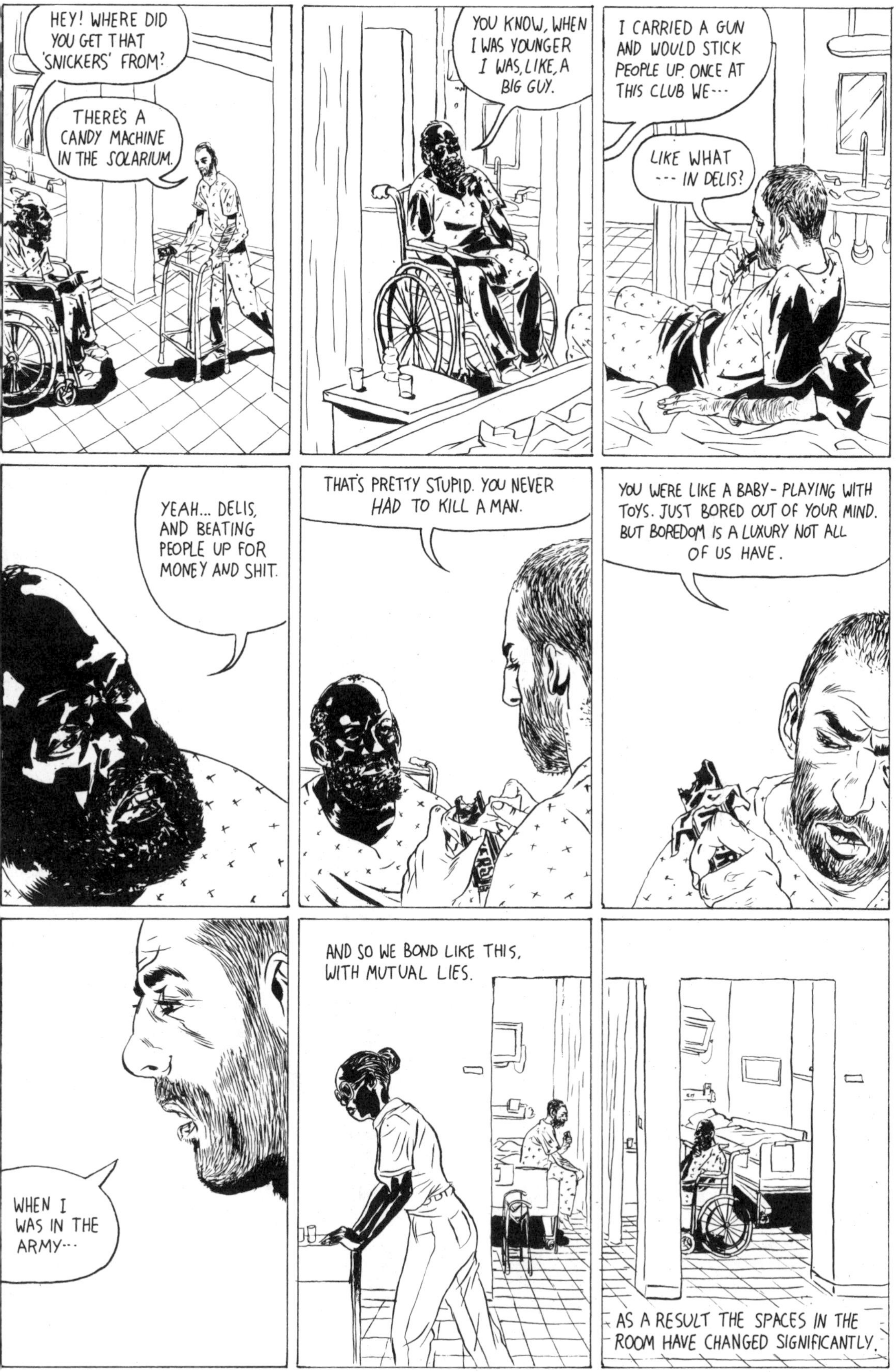
HEY! WHERE DID YOU GET THAT 'SNICKERS' FROM?
THERE'S A CANDY MACHINE IN THE SOLARIUM.
YOU KNOW, WHEN I WAS YOUNGER I WAS, LIKE, A BIG GUY.
I CARRIED A GUN AND WOULD STICK PEOPLE UP. ONCE AT THIS CLUB WE---
LIKE WHAT --- IN DELIS?
YEAH... DELIS, AND BEATING PEOPLE UP FOR MONEY AND SHIT.
THAT'S PRETTY STUPID. YOU NEVER HAD TO KILL A MAN.
YOU WERE LIKE A BABY- PLAYING WITH TOYS. JUST BORED OUT OF YOUR MIND. BUT BOREDOM IS A LUXURY NOT ALL OF US HAVE.
WHEN I WAS IN THE ARMY---
AND SO WE BOND LIKE THIS, WITH MUTUAL LIES.
AS A RESULT THE SPACES IN THE ROOM HAVE CHANGED SIGNIFICANTLY.

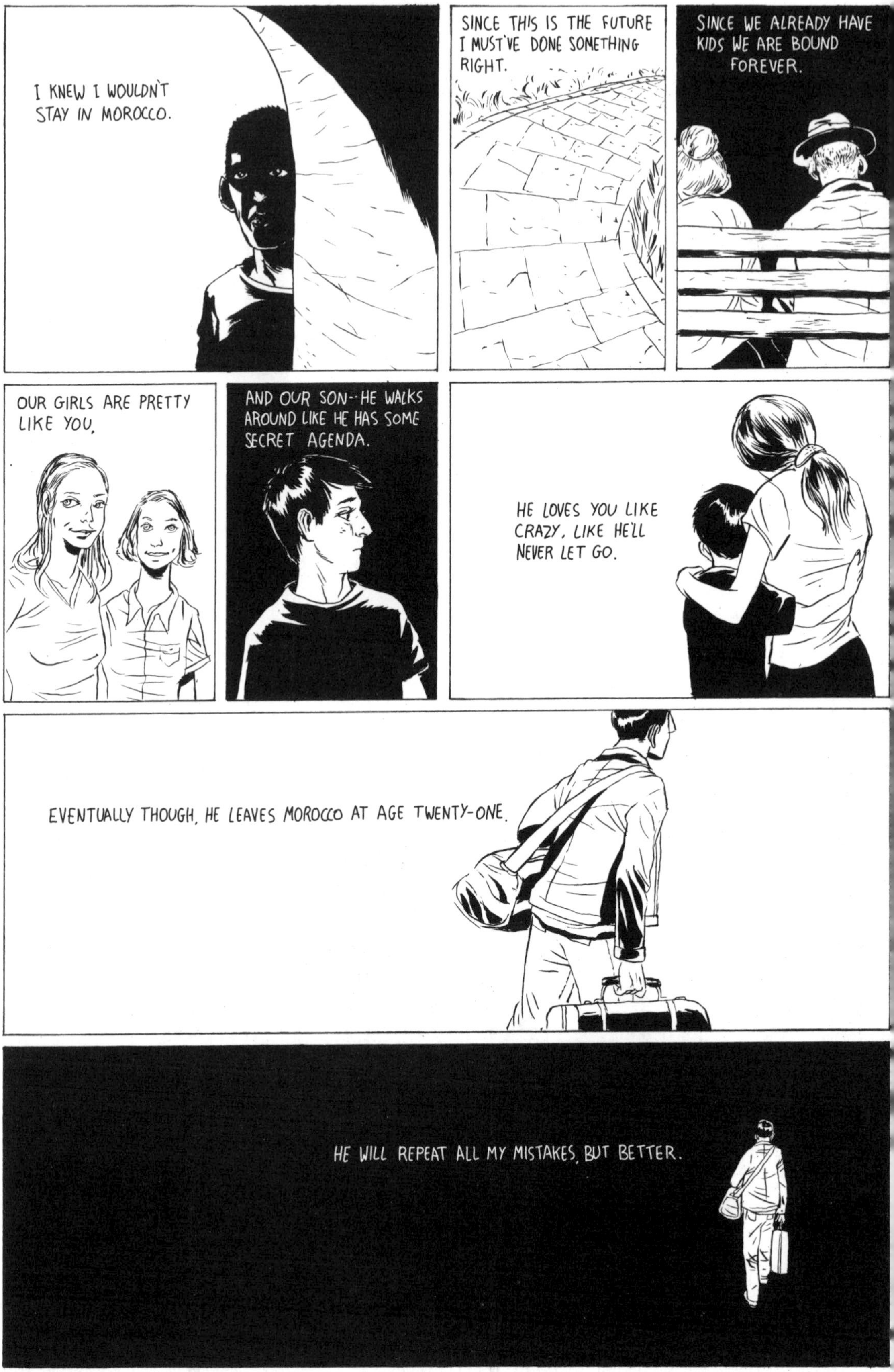

I KNEW I WOULDN'T STAY IN MOROCCO.
SINCE THIS IS THE FUTURE I MUST'VE DONE SOMETHING RIGHT.
SINCE WE ALREADY HAVE KIDS WE ARE BOUND FOREVER.
OUR GIRLS ARE PRETTY LIKE YOU,
AND OUR SON-- HE WALKS AROUND LIKE HE HAS SOME SECRET AGENDA.
HE LOVES YOU LIKE CRAZY, LIKE HE'LL NEVER LET GO.
EVENTUALLY THOUGH, HE LEAVES MOROCCO AT AGE TWENTY-ONE.
HE WILL REPEAT ALL MY MISTAKES, BUT BETTER.

HE WILL SETTLE DOWN IN A PLACE WHERE HE CAN'T SPEAK THE LOCAL LANGUAGE,

AND WILL GET BY ON KILLER CHARISMA AND MAMA'S BOY EYES.

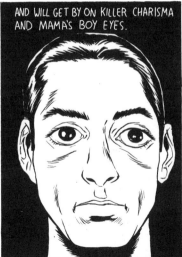

OUR DAUGHTERS WILL NEVER LEAVE US OR EACH OTHER.

ONE OF THEM WILL EVEN MARRY AN IMMIGRANT.

AND THE GUY THAT FUCKED YOU IN HIGH SCHOOL —

IS STILL SITTING IN MY LIVING ROOM, YAKKING AWAY. I THINK HE KNOWS I KNOW.

HE KISSED YOU 'HELLO' WHEN HE CAME IN.

MEANWHILE OUR FUTURE SON IS TAKING A FOREIGN CITY BY STORM.

HE IS INFUSED WITH THAT UNTOUCHABLE AMBITION THAT DEFIES CYNICISM.

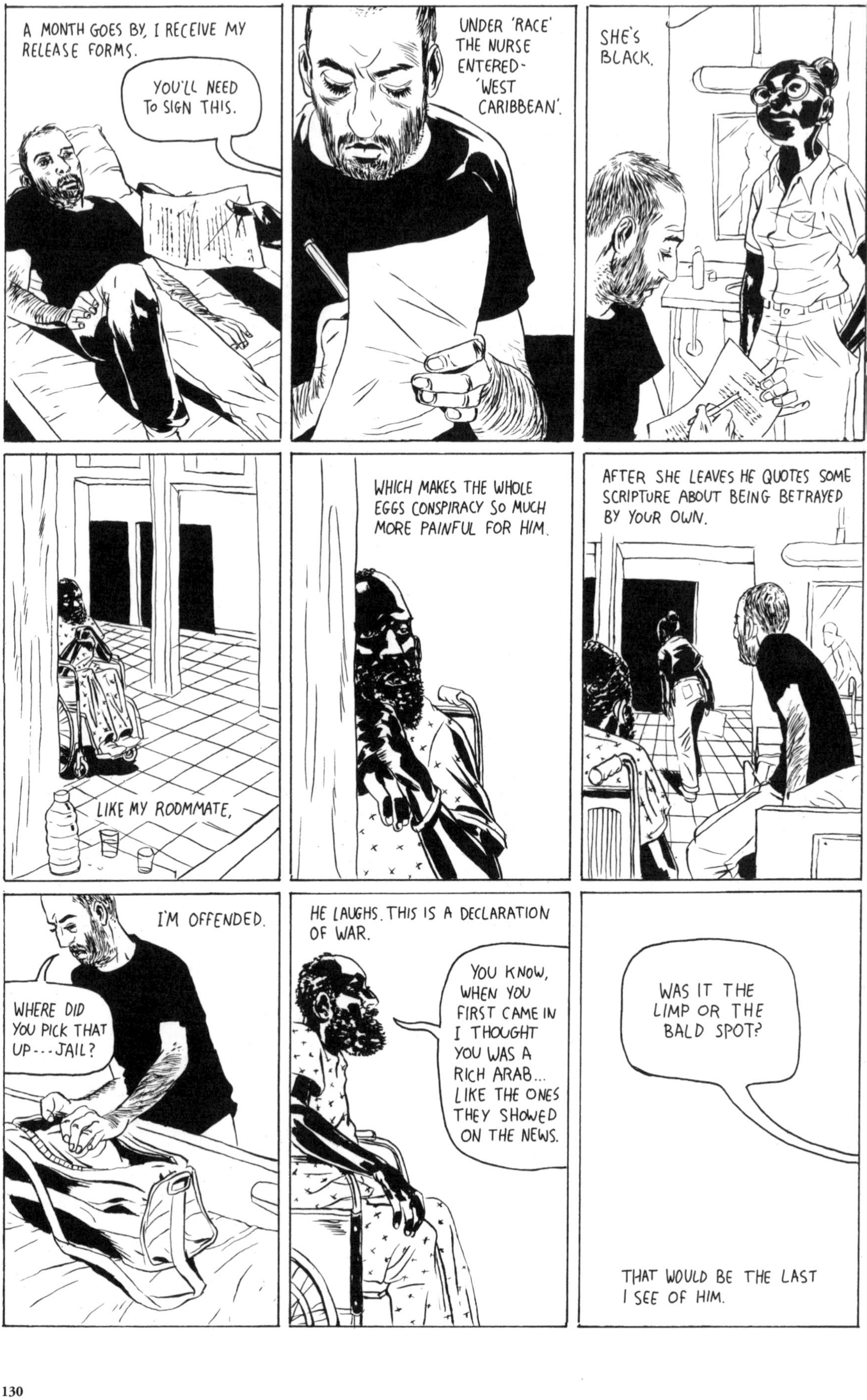
A MONTH GOES BY, I RECEIVE MY RELEASE FORMS.
YOU'LL NEED TO SIGN THIS.
UNDER 'RACE' THE NURSE ENTERED- 'WEST CARIBBEAN'.
SHE'S BLACK.
LIKE MY ROOMMATE,
WHICH MAKES THE WHOLE EGGS CONSPIRACY SO MUCH MORE PAINFUL FOR HIM.
AFTER SHE LEAVES HE QUOTES SOME SCRIPTURE ABOUT BEING BETRAYED BY YOUR OWN.
I'M OFFENDED.
WHERE DID YOU PICK THAT UP---JAIL?
HE LAUGHS. THIS IS A DECLARATION OF WAR.
YOU KNOW, WHEN YOU FIRST CAME IN I THOUGHT YOU WAS A RICH ARAB... LIKE THE ONES THEY SHOWED ON THE NEWS.
WAS IT THE LIMP OR THE BALD SPOT?
THAT WOULD BE THE LAST I SEE OF HIM.

I HAD A FEELING ALL OF THIS WOULD HAPPEN THE FIRST TIME I SAW YOU.

THAT WAS RIGHT AFTER YOU GOT YELLED AT BY YOUR MOM. YOU WERE FOUR OR FIVE.

A LITTLE GIRL LOOKING AT THE SUNSET, KNOWING NOTHING REALLY MATTERS.

A WISE LITTLE GIRL WITH KILLER CHARISMA.

I DIDN'T KNOW YOU THEN, BUT YOU KNOW WHAT I MEAN.

I JUST KNEW YOU EXISTED.

I ENDED UP IN MOROCCO, BUT IT WAS NO ACCIDENT. I COULD SPEAK THE LOCAL LANGUAGE. I WAS THIRTY FOUR.

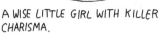

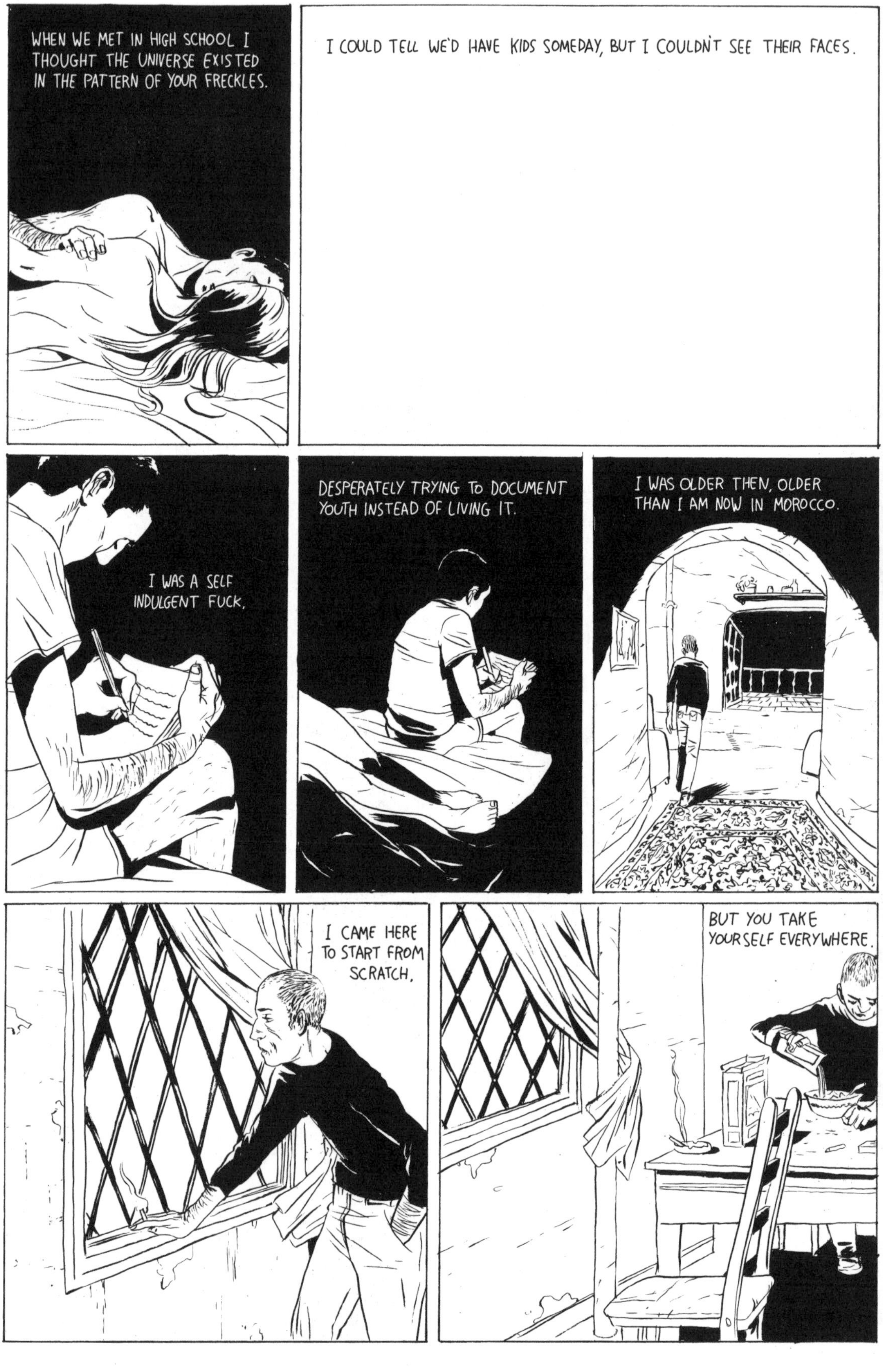
WHEN WE MET IN HIGH SCHOOL I THOUGHT THE UNIVERSE EXISTED IN THE PATTERN OF YOUR FRECKLES.
I COULD TELL WE'D HAVE KIDS SOMEDAY, BUT I COULDN'T SEE THEIR FACES.
I WAS A SELF INDULGENT FUCK,
DESPERATELY TRYING TO DOCUMENT YOUTH INSTEAD OF LIVING IT.
I WAS OLDER THEN, OLDER THAN I AM NOW IN MOROCCO.
I CAME HERE TO START FROM SCRATCH,
BUT YOU TAKE YOURSELF EVERYWHERE.

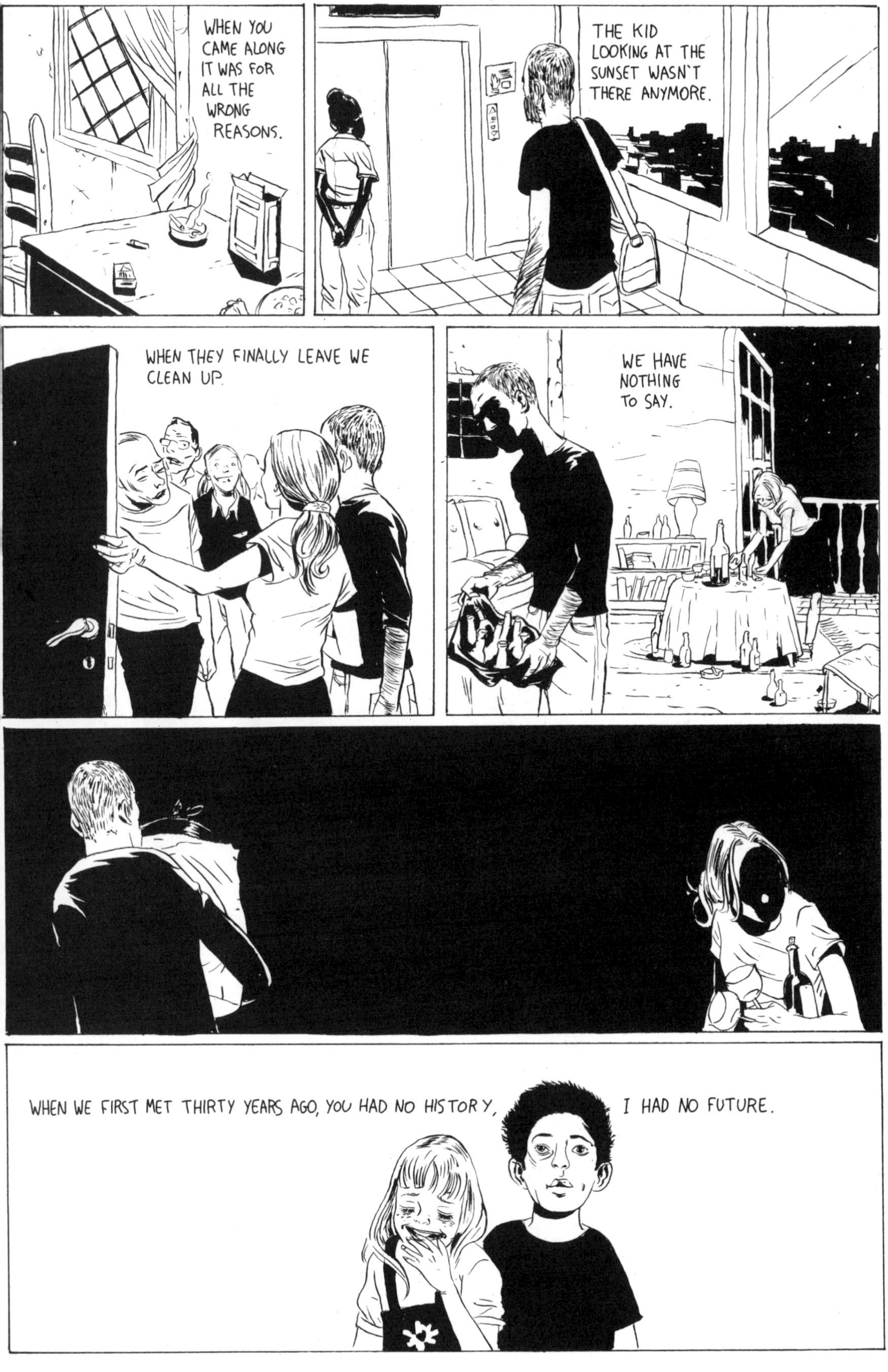
WHEN YOU CAME ALONG IT WAS FOR ALL THE WRONG REASONS.
THE KID LOOKING AT THE SUNSET WASN'T THERE ANYMORE.
WHEN THEY FINALLY LEAVE WE CLEAN UP.
WE HAVE NOTHING TO SAY.
WHEN WE FIRST MET THIRTY YEARS AGO, YOU HAD NO HISTORY,
I HAD NO FUTURE.